Marie Osmond's Collector Dolls

The First Ten Years

Marie Osmond's Collector Dolls

The First Ten Years

Text by Nayda Rondon

Photography by Tamas D. Kish

Portfolio Press

First Edition/First Printing

Copyright © 2001 Marie, Inc. and Portfolio Press Corporation. All rights reserved. No part of the contents of this book may be reproduced without the written permission of the publisher.

To purchase additional copies of this book, please contact: Portfolio Press, 130 Wineow St., Cumberland, MD 21502. 877-737-1200

Library of Congress Catalog Card Number 2001-130309

ISBN 0-942620-52-6

Project Editor: Krystyna Poray Goddu
Designed by John Peace Design

Cover photo by Merrett Smith and Newman Photography
Back cover photos of Helena and Olive May by Tamas D. Kish
Marie Osmond's personal photos reprinted courtesy of Marie Osmond

Printed and bound in Korea

Contents

Dear Fellow Collectors and Doll Enthusiasts,

I can't believe it! Ten years! It seems like just yesterday when I was choosing the fabrics and sculpts for my first dolls, which debuted on QVC and in the Disney theme parks, in the summer of 1991. You know the cliché, "Time flies when you're having fun!"...well, my doll line is absolute, living proof of it!

We chose the "Remember Me" theme for our Tenth Year Anniversary because I have so many wonderful memories from the past decade. First and foremost are my fellow collectors. You are the reason we began ten years ago; you are the reason we are still here today; and you are the reason we plan to be here for many years, and many memories to come! As I meet with you and read your kind letters and emails, I carry a part of you with me. Your stories and passion for collecting invigorate me, and serve to strengthen my resolve to continue sharing my own passion. There is something very special about collectors. They have heart; they have purpose; they have passion!

At the risk of omitting events that should have been included, I'd like to name a few of my fondest memories over the past ten years.

- My debut appearance on QVC with Mary Beth Roe. I was so nervous and excited... all at the same time.
- The honorary parade through Disney World with one of my first dolls, Jessica, (named after my oldest daughter) and then putting her hands in cement at the MGM Theater.
- Being honored as the first human ever to appear on the cover of *Doll Reader* magazine.
- The night from you-know-where in the Atlanta airport en route to Philadelphia for a QVC show. (I won't go into detail, but trust me...it was memorable!)
- Every time I've sculpted! Each doll I've created has unique circumstances.
- Attending Toy Fair for the first time. I was blown away at the magnitude of it all!
- My Fifth Anniversary on QVC. I collaborated with the wonderful Annette Funicello on a doll and teddy bear vignette entitled, I Love You Beary Much. Annette's declining health prohibited her from being there personally, but she called while I was on the air, and in her faint voice told me, "I love you beary much!" What a thrill! And then, my parents walked on stage to surprise me. I had no idea they were there! What a memory.
- My first sculpt, Olive May, selling out in the midnight hour on QVC. You'll read more about that event in the book, but I had to mention it. What a night!
- Driving with Lisa Hatch and Lou Knickerbocker from Fayetteville to Bentonville, Arkansas, to present a new doll concept to Wal-Mart, when the back of the van popped open while we were speeding down the highway, spilling our one and only product samples out onto the road. We yelled at Lou to stop the car. Lisa and I jumped out and frantically went about picking up the dolls—all the time Lou was shouting at us, trying to warn us of the very large oncoming semi-truck! I think we "aged" Lou that night, but we retrieved all the samples!
- My broken toe, the chicken salad, and my luggage at Lane's Toyland.
- Hiding from the press and sneaking in after-hours at Enchanted Cottage.
- The size of the warehouse, the spa and the long lines at The Doll Market.
- Karl's new shoes and sore feet at FAO Schwarz.
- The limo driver who, while driving us from the airport to our hotel on a doll signing trip, made what looked to us to be a drug trade on a back road in the middle of nowhere, while we sat petrified in the back of the car.
- The hospitality of the MGM Grand in Las Vegas.
- The "special trips" with my kids, coconut macaroons with Martha Blanding and pin trading at the Disney signings.
- More special trips with my kids and hearing first hand from collectors how much they loved our Wizard of Oz product at the Warner Bros. signing.

- The amount of dolls, the nice aroma, and the great gift packages at Buffalo Candle.
- At any signing, meeting the collectors, hearing their stories, sharing their passion.
- The trips to QVC-UK, meeting the British collectors, shopping at Harrods and our nightly ritual of hot chocolate in the hotel lobby.
- Going to QVC-Germany and having to use a translator on air to communicate and Karl, my manager, playing Colonel Klink and making me very nervous as I tried to distance myself from him.
- Receiving my first DOTY nominations for Adora Belle, Peek-A-Boo and Elise.
- I'll never forget the night Adora Belle debuted on QVC. It seemed the entire world was glued to their television sets as the horrible news of Lady Diana's crash was announced. I, too, watched in the Green Room waiting for updates and praying for the best. Just moments before I was to step on stage, the announcement was made that she had died. Mary Beth and I looked at each other, and with heavy hearts, (and really still in shock over it) wondered how on earth we could go on air after such a tragedy. Unfortunately for us, with live T.V., the show must go on, so we went through the motions for the next hour on air, but our hearts and minds were somewhere else.
- The pandemonium in the Green Room at QVC just two hours before we were to debut our vinyl Beauty Bugs. My daughter, Rachael, Lisa's daughter, Alexis, Tammy Knickerbocker's daughter, Lindsay, and Marie D'Amore's daughter, Christina, were supposed to wear matching costumes, until we discovered just hours before the show that two of the costumes hadn't been made! With no time to waste, we all jumped in to make them. We used anything we could find...staples, glue guns, duct tape, magic markers, hangers, styrofoam, super glue...even a sewing machine...and voila! All four Beauty Bugs were ready for their television debut! What an event! What a memory! What a mess we made in the Green Room!

It's impossible to thank everyone who has contributed, in any way, to my doll line over the past ten years, and because I'm sure I'll leave someone out, I'm not even going to try. I, do, however want to give sincere thanks to Mr. Lou Knickerbocker for dreaming big and giving me a great opportunity. His passion gave wings to my passion. Thanks, also, to Marty Krasner, a natural born leader with great vision, integrity and heart.

Thanks to Lisa Hatch, Karl Engemann, Allen Finlinson, Steve Hortin and Kesti Poulsen for their invaluable contributions to my doll line. From the very beginning, these friends and associates of mine have worked with me for a combined total of over eighty years!

I do want to thank those who worked so diligently to make this book a reality, which has been a dream of mine for many years.

- Thanks to Robert Rowe, Krystyna Goddu and Nayda Rondon at Portfolio Press. You've given me and my collectors a great gift!
- Thanks to L.L. Knickerbocker and QVC for believing in this project enough to put their money where my mouth was!
- Thanks to Tamas Kish for his talent and patience. (I owe you some more Krispy Kremes!)
- Thanks to Kesti Poulsen for spearheading this overwhelming project! Without Kesti, there would be no book!
- Thanks to Karen Seamons and her entire "crew" (Karen Dursteller, Ashlie Hansen, Heidi Sass, Joyce and William McDonell...and you, too, Ron!) for letting us invade your home and life to help facilitate this project.
- Thanks to all the sculptors and costume designers who have shared their talents with me for the past ten years. Without their contributions, this book truly wouldn't be possible.
- Thanks to Toni Brown, Bonnie McMullin, Devyn Brown, Merrett Smith, Dave and Mike Newman, David and Lori Mesnard, Joshua Hawkes, Tyler Hortin, Beverly Carlson, Bonni Myszka, for your invaluable contributions.

Ten years...WOW! And as good as it's been, I believe the best is yet to come! Thanks for all the memories, and for sharing your passion!

Love,

A LIFELONG LOVE AFFAIR WITH DOLLS

Marie Osmond has endeared herself to millions of loyal fans throughout the world ever since her debut on *The Andy Williams Show* at the tender age of three. A true international celebrity, she's enjoyed the highest levels of success in almost every field of entertainment for thirty-eight years.

These days, though, when you encounter some of her loyal devotees, they're as likely to be admirers of her doll line, eagerly awaiting each new creation with all the anticipation her earlier fans showed at the release of her latest hit record. Whether it's through her songs, her stage, movie and television roles, her efforts as a child advocate or her work as head of the Marie Osmond Fine Porcelain Collector Doll Line, Marie's sincere commitment to what she's doing, and her appreciation and love of people, shine through. She's a woman of strong emotions and convictions who packs her enthusiasm into everything she does, particularly her doll line.

"I'm pretty energetic when it comes to living," she says, with a laugh that invites you to join in. "I don't do anything half-heartedly, let's put it that way. My doll line is not just my business; it's my passion. It gives me a creative outlet, and brings my love of children and dolls together."

Indeed, her lifelong love affair with dolls started in the cradle—literally. She was born on October 13, 1959, in Ogden, Utah, and by Christmas, her mom—ecstatic at finally having given birth to a daughter—was already busy picking out a doll to leave under the tree. "I couldn't wait to buy her a doll," Marie's mother, Olive Osmond, recalls with a chuckle. "I went right out and I got her a little vinyl doll for that first Christmas."

Mrs. Osmond's excitement was easy to understand. As the only girl in a family of nine children, Marie provided her mom with the perfect excuse to indulge in her own passion for dolls, and much to their mutual delight, she went about "inundating" Marie with dolls.

"Her first baby doll was named Bubbles," Mrs. Osmond chronicles. "When she was very little and just learning to talk, Marie had a lisp. Her father would tease her, asking her whether her doll's name was Sugar, pronouncing it as 'Thugar' and she'd very earnestly shake her head and say 'no, Fatha, it's Bubbelths,' and hug the doll." To little Marie, the doll clearly had an identity and personality, and she couldn't understand why grownups like her father seemed to have such a difficult time grasping the concept.

Marie's next doll did not receive the same type of treatment, however. As her mother relates, no sooner had she given it to Marie than the little girl went about "personalizing" it by drawing all over the face. Marie was only a toddler, but it seems she was already determined to leave her artistic mark on dolls!

For the most part, though, Marie was very loving with, and protective of her dolls, developing strong attachments to particular ones. First there was a favorite play doll that Marie liked to take to the drive-in movies. Then there was Thumbelina. "She had quite a few dolls by this time and I couldn't understand what her fascination was for this ugly little doll that squirmed when you pulled her cord," Mrs. Osmond says. "I asked her once, 'Why do you love this doll so much?' And she answered, 'Because I feel sorry for her. Who else would buy her…she needs me!'"

Marie's sensitive nature and active imagination found a happy outlet in her doll play. "That's one of the things about being an only girl—I did a lot of one-on-one play with my dolls," Marie notes. "I went everywhere with them, and it just wasn't one. I always had two or three in my arms. Doll playing fosters a great and creative imagination."

Not that she didn't have a lot of other creative resources to draw upon—she had a whole family of them! Her father, George Virl Osmond, was a gifted amateur singer who wooed and won Marie's mom with his voice and dancing talents. Her mother's artistic tendencies led her to playing the saxophone in a dance band, sewing and fashion. In between being a full-time mom to her growing brood of children, she enjoyed taking clothing-design classes, and even commissioned sculpts of modeling dolls to help her fit her designs. And of course, there were Marie's brothers. Although the two oldest boys—Virl and Tom—were hearing-impaired and thus not part of the performing group, Marie's other siblings—Alan, Wayne, Merrill and Jay—made up the Osmond Brothers, a singing group that rose to national fame on *The Andy Williams Show*.

Growing up in a family of strong religious and moral beliefs, who also happened to be household names, Marie spent an interesting and eventful childhood. Her early years represented a unique dichotomy that would greatly influence

her character. In one sense, her childhood was filled with basic values and ordinary everyday occurrences. On another level, it was interspersed with extraordinary happenings, famous and artistic people, and far-ranging travel. As the Osmond Brothers toured throughout the world, the younger siblings and their mother would sometimes accompany them. "From the time I was very young, I was around costume and set designers, makeup artists and creative people of all kinds," Marie says. The bright little girl absorbed much, unconsciously storing her observations for use years later, when it came to designing her own doll line. Marie also made the most of her travels. She and her mom had a great time buying dolls from the various countries they visited. By age seven, Marie was firmly hooked on collecting dolls. "I really loved collecting, but I became passionate about it after I received my first porcelain doll," she relates. "Porcelain dolls are beautiful; they're very realistic and I love the weight of them. It makes a little girl feel she has to be a bit more gentle and loving."

Back home she continued collecting porcelain dolls and became very interested in twins. Later, she became the proud collector of about 100 Barbies and friends, and started to add Madame Alexander dolls to her enviable collection, which today numbers well over 700, in addition to the dolls in her own line. Ruled by her heartstrings, it was an eclectic mix comprised mostly of brides, babies and twins. "I had everything from play vinyl to porcelain," Marie says. "But after several years, it wasn't about play anymore. My mother and I both loved dolls, and it helped to further

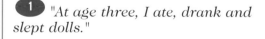

1 *"At age three, I ate, drank and slept dolls."*

2 *"To get Donny and Jimmy to play Barbies, I had to learn to play Legos. I could build a mean tower!"*

3 *"Once mother and I got the pattern down, we made costumes for the whole family!"*

bond us…especially in my teenage years!

"It doesn't matter how old you are—dolls transcend all ages, and that's one of the reasons that I loved—and still love—collecting dolls," Marie continues. "It's something that grandmothers can do with granddaughters, aunts can do with their nieces, mothers can do with their teenagers, and teenage girls can have in common with their little sisters."

"Marie and I are very close," Mrs. Osmond agrees. "We did a lot of things together while George traveled with the older boys."

Sewing was one of those mother-daughter activities. Crediting these craft sessions as one of her earliest design and fashion influences, Marie remembers her mother sewing dresses for her and her dolls. Marie would sit and watch while her mother worked. Pretty soon, she was sewing right alongside. By age ten, she was so adept with the sewing machine that she was making her own skirts, blouses and pajamas. "Marie was always very artistic," her mother says. "When she was around ten or twelve years old, we took a dress-designing course together from a man who used to design beautiful gowns for the stars. He took me to the side once and asked whether I was sure Marie had never done this type of thing before because she was doing such a marvelous job. She just had a flair for design and color. It came naturally to her."

Another popular pastime for Marie was playing with brother Donny, who was also too young at the time to join the Osmond Brothers group. When the youngest Osmond, Jimmy, joined the family, he was recruited as a playmate as well.

"Growing up with eight brothers, I had to learn multi-interests just to survive," Marie relates. "I would play army soldiers, football and do all the guy stuff, and then I'd cleverly convince Donny and Jimmy to play Barbies with me. Donny had a Ken doll, and Jimmy had a Ricky doll."

"They had so much fun," Mrs. Osmond reminisces, telling how her children would spend hours playing at show business by building sets, and producing songs and skits that they would then act out with their dolls. Marie always insisted on being the one to design the clothes for these lavish productions.

Those early play rehearsals were great preparation for what was to become a life in the spotlight. Marie was only three years old when she appeared on *The Andy Williams Show* in 1963. When Andy introduced her as the "youngest Osmond Brother," the viewers found her hard to resist as she sat on Andy's lap and flashed that trademark smile. Ten years later, Marie was back on the entertainment scene in a big way: The thirteen-year-old made country music history as the first female artist to debut with

a number-one cross-over hit; "Paper Roses" was number one country and number five pop. She went on to earn a gold record, as well as Grammy nominations for Best Female Country Vocal Performance and Best New Artist. Not long after, she hit the live concert stage with a sold-out performance at New York City's Madison Square Garden alongside the Osmond Brothers. In a demonstration of practical chivalry—not to mention accuracy—the group's name was changed to The Osmonds when she went on the road with them.

From there, it was one success topped by another. After the *Paper Roses* album, she released *My Little Corner of the World* (1974) and *Who's Sorry Now* (1975). From 1974–79, she teamed up with brother Donny to star in ABC's television hit, *The Donny and Marie Show*, which aired in more than forty countries internationally. In doing so, Donny, then sixteen, and Marie, then fourteen, became the youngest-ever hosts of a weekly prime-time variety show. The idols of millions, the siblings were a national sensation. Donny was the one the girls wanted to date, and Marie was the one they wanted to emulate, right down to her trend-setting haircuts and fashions.

During and after the hit variety show she starred in several television movies, including *The Gift of Love* (1979) with James Woods and Timothy

4 *"Here I am at twelve years old recording my first #1 hit, "Paper Roses." The airline lost my luggage, so my mother came to the rescue and purchased me a few necessities—clothes, a toothbrush and a new doll!"*

5 *"Donny and I dressed for one of our comedy sketches on the original* Donny and Marie Show—*look who's sitting behind the smile! (Ha-Ha)"*

6 *"My father said it would never happen, but here I am posing with my modeling doll. My mother loved watching him eat the chocolate version!"*

7 *"Here's Donny and me during the original* Donny and Marie Show, *with two of our favorite on-air guests, our parents."*

Bottoms; *Side by Side: The Story of the Osmond Family* (1982) in which she played her mother; and *I Married Wyatt Earp* (1983) with Bruce Boxleitner. There was also a stint in 1985 as co-host of the television series *Ripley's Believe It or Not*. But for the most part, her singing continued to dominate. In 1985, she recorded *There's No Stopping Your Heart,* which featured two number-one country hits—the title track and "Meet Me in Montana," a duet with Dan Seals that won the Country Music Association's (CMA) Vocal Duo of the Year award. In 1986, another duet—this time with Paul Davis—from the *I Only Wanted You* album, earned her a CMA Vocal Duo of the Year nomination for the number-one country hit "You're Still New to Me." Two other albums followed: *All in Love* (1988) and *Steppin' Stone* (1989), as did a 1989 nomination by the Academy of Country Music for Top Female Vocalist.

She took to the road with *Marie Osmond's The Magic of Christmas* show, as well as to play Maria in the national touring company production of Rodgers and Hammerstein's *The Sound of Music* (1994–95), a role she reprised on a Southeast Asia tour in the summer of 1997. That same year, she realized a personal dream, when she made her Broadway debut as Anna in Rodgers and Hammerstein's *The King and I.* "Preparing for Broadway was one of the most challenging feats I've tackled in my entertainment career. I had grown up on television and singing on stage as 'Marie Osmond,' so that came natural to me. With theatre, however, I had to learn to speak and sing dif-

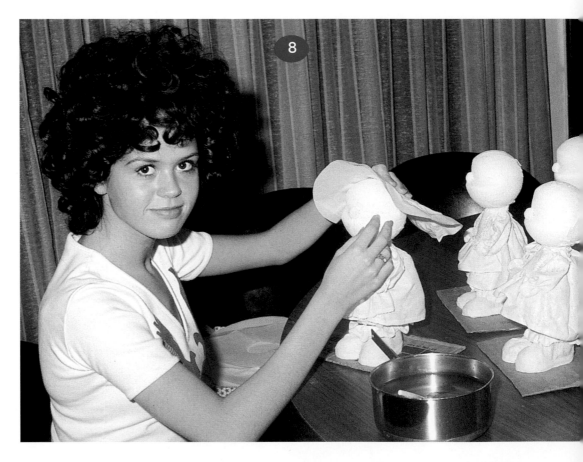

ferently, to act differently on stage, to become someone else, to memorize a three-hour play, and the real trick…to take a lead personality from a much-beloved play and movie and make it 'mine.' And, due to my crazy schedule at the time, I had to do it all in three weeks! I don't remember ever working so hard. Perhaps that's why opening night on Broadway, at the Neil Simon Theatre, was so rewarding for me…because it took so much personal effort to get there." In the spring of 1998, Marie headlined the play's national touring production in San Francisco and Los Angeles.

Sharing many of Marie's professional and personal highs and lows throughout these years has been Lisa Hatch, Marie's close friend and right-hand woman in the doll business. The two first met in 1985, when a mutual friend introduced them after one of Marie's concert performances. Looking back today, neither can recall any earth-shattering conversation or "signs" of what was to come, but both do agree that they experienced a comfortable sense of "clicking" with one another.

A week after they met, Lisa received a call from Marie's business manager, Allen Finlinson, offering her a job as Marie's wardrobe assistant. Lisa, a corporate secretary at the time, took a leap of faith, and accepted. ("I didn't have a clue as to what one does for a celebrity," Lisa confesses. "Would I be making nail appointments for her all day, or what?") Hardly! Today, as creative director for the Marie Osmond

Fine Porcelain Collector Doll Line, Lisa is an integral part of Marie's inner doll circle. "She calls me her brain, but I don't take credit (or blame) for that! I'm her vice president of 'stuff,' her facilitator." Lisa laughs. "She's the collector; I'm not. I'm more concerned with the details and the ins-and-outs on the logistics side. I guess you could say that we're the left and right sides of the brain, but then again, we cross over even as we complement each other."

A sense of humor also forms a strong bond between the two. In just one example of the many inside jokes the two friends share, Lisa relates, "On

our first trip to the airport together after being hired, I remember Marie turning to me and saying, 'You have great hair!' I heard it as, 'grey' hair, and because I do have a few grey hairs, I quickly responded, 'You're right, I do,' all the time thinking to myself, 'Wow, what a tart!' Of course, Marie, knowing what she had said, heard my response and thought, 'Wow, what a tart!' It's a testament to our friendship that we got past this awkward first impression. In fact, it wasn't until six years later that we re-lived the moment, finally realizing the misunderstanding and laughing our heads off! Now, sixteen years later, we both have *great* hair!"

8 *"Give me a few empty soda bottles and voila! I'll turn them into a doll! I was sixteen or seventeen when I created these Dip n' Drape dolls to give to my family members and girlfriends."*

9 *"From a young age, I enjoyed dolls of all mediums. What else would a girl do with her empty panty hose 'eggs' but turn them into dolls?"*

10 *"Mother and I took a design and draping class from George Trippon when I was thirteen years old. Here I am working with a half-size figure, where I first learned to drape fabric. We had too much fun!"*

KNICKERBOCKER COMES KNOCKING

Throughout her entertainment career, Marie continued to amass her doll collection and, more importantly, the skills and talents that would serve her well in her future efforts as a doll designer. "Making dolls is bringing music and painting and entertainment to another dimension," asserts Marie, who is also an amateur painter.

The essential elements for Marie's successful entry into the doll world were clearly there. All that was needed was the opportunity. It came knocking in the form of businessman Lou Knickerbocker. After reading an article about Marie that touched upon her love of dolls, Lou approached her with an intriguing proposition—to partner with the L. L. Knickerbocker Company in developing a line of fine porcelain dolls. She loved the idea, but was adamant about being more than a celebrity figurehead. She wanted to be intimately involved in all aspects of the creative process. "When Lou came to me and asked whether I'd endorse a line of dolls, I said, 'I'll tell you what, Lou, I'm not interested in endorsing. I'm interested in designing,'" Marie says. "I think he was a little panicked initially because he thought, 'Oh, brother, what does she know about it?' But I had grown up around some of the best designers in the business. I explained to him that I had designed some of my clothes growing up, even creating patterns under my name for the Butterick Pattern Company at one point, and that, as part of my entertainment background, I'd developed a good sense of color, fashion and fabrics," Marie says. "On top of all that, I was a serious doll collector, so, I knew what collectors might be looking for."

It didn't take much convincing. Marie began designing dolls for the L. L. Knickerbocker Company in 1990, debuting the brand in August 1991. To date the company has created more than 500 dolls in the Marie Osmond Fine Porcelain Collector Doll Line.

When Marie said she wanted to be an active participant, she wasn't kidding. Although at first she didn't sculpt any of the dolls herself, from day one she did take a very hands-on approach to conceptualizing and designing all of the dolls in the collection. One of her key strengths lay in knowing how to bring all the elements together. Her show business experience had taught her that it takes a team of talented and caring people to achieve a product of quality. Whether she was involved in creating a record album, a televi-

sion show or a doll, Marie recognized that producing a hit of any kind required collaborative teamwork. "There are a lot of artistic, wonderful sculptors and creative people who don't like to be bothered with the business side," Marie explains. "I know wonderful sculptors who prefer not to costume, and I know fabulous designers who create wonderful costumes but don't sculpt faces."

Consequently, Marie began to gather a team of talented doll sculptors, costumers, and marketing and business associates to help bring her visions to reality. "I think what's great about our little group is that we each have a different eye. So, as a whole, we succeed at providing something that is not only beautiful and has an appealing concept, but is also of high quality and cost-effective."

What's perhaps most unique about Marie's work style is that it's anything but conventional. Martin Krasner, L. L. Knickerbocker's Chief Executive Officer and Acting President, recalls that one of his earliest memories of Marie is of meeting her with a cadre of lawyers and business people on the set of her daytime show after a long day of taping. The meeting lasted for several hours and Marie was sharp, focused and professional throughout it. What most impressed Martin, however, was that she conducted the entire conference with a little baby in her arms. "I really admire her commitment to her family and how she manages to fit it all in," he says. "She's amazing! Since then, every time I see Marie, she always has one of her children with her."

Speaking for herself and the rest of her core group of business intimates, Marie says: "I think all of our families are really supportive. I *know* Allen's family is supportive. After all, his wife, Breta Finlinson, helps create many costumes for my line. Breta loves working on the small dolls,

11

and she doesn't miss a detail. If you love my Greeting Card line, or my Petite Amour line or my Bunny Love line—then you love Breta's work! If you have to work, it's a great way to make a living," Marie continues. "There are stressful times, but it's that way with anything you do. I can't think of anything more fun—and I've done a lot of fun things in my life."

The elements of novelty and surprise are part of what make her adventures in the doll world so enjoyable. Take doll

signings, for instance. Marie never knows what will happen at one of these events.

"At my doll signings, I try not to make it just, 'Hi, let me sign your doll; you're out of here.' There are so many people that we do have to move the line relatively quickly, but I'm sorry—I like talking to people and learning about their lives and listening to their doll stories. I'm also a little hypoglycemic, so I have to take an occasional break and have a little protein. I can't go four-and-a-half hours without having to go to the bathroom, either. Well, at one of my signings a charmingly outspoken woman waited in the first line, then she waited in the second line, while I continued talking, telling stories and signing

dolls. Finally, it was her turn at the front of the line. With bags of dolls in her weary arms, she walked right up to me and said, 'Sit down, shut up, don't you dare go to the bathroom—just sign my dolls!' Everybody within the sound of her voice started cracking up. It was hysterical!"

On another occasion, Marie broke her toe on the way to a doll signing at Lane's Toyland in Texarkana, Arkansas. "It was killing me. I couldn't believe I'd broken it," Marie recounts. "We got on the flight, and my foot started swelling so badly I couldn't wear my shoe. By the time we got to the signing, I had to keep my foot elevated. My four-inch, high-heeled fashion boots I'd brought to match my outfit no longer fit my swollen foot, so I had to wear a pair of slip-on flat shoes that didn't come close to matching my outfit. I'm sure people were looking at me and thinking, 'You're a doll designer? You can't even dress yourself!' It was a huge fashion no-no."

Unperturbed, Marie, who likes to be as close as possible to her fans, sat out in the open making no effort to hide her injured toe and fashion faux pas. "I had my leg extended and elevated on a box, when Sue Rogers, co-owner of Lane's Toyland, introduced me to a man who would become 'the hero' of the day—Dr. Glen Feeback. What are the odds of there being a foot specialist at my doll signing, and me with a broken toe! He generously went back to his office to get supplies, and then returned to treat my foot, even putting ice on it. What a guy, and what a memory!"

"I think the reason that this doll line is still here and thriving after ten years is because of the collectors," Lisa comments. "Obviously, we wouldn't be here without them. But what's so intriguing to me is that when we go to signings, people always come up and marvel, 'Wow, she really looks like she enjoys this.' Well, she really does enjoy it! It's not something that she does simply to promote the dolls."

"She is incredible with her fans," attests Sue Rogers. Marie, known for being extremely loyal, has been going to yearly doll signings at Sue's store ever since she hit it off with Sue and her

11 *"I want every doll to be perfect, just like the original prototype."*

husband, Alan, at the American International Toy Fair in 1995.

"Her first signing with us was in 1996, and it was incredible. That first year we had pre-sold over 2,000 dolls and Marie came one afternoon at 5:30 p.m. and she signed until 1 a.m.! It was unbelievable how she joked and signed the whole way through without a single complaint. Then she came back the next day to sign for the public. Her scheduled appearance was from 10 a.m. to 2 p.m., but she stayed until 4 p.m. and almost missed her flight. She is so gracious and attentive to everyone."

If there are children in line at any of her appearances, you can bet that Marie will sit them on her lap and make them feel extra special. "It never fails," says Sue. "She will stop everything to take that extra time with a little child. She absolutely adores children, and they her."

As much as possible, Marie makes it a point to combine her doll pursuits with her truest love—her children. "We'll go to doll signings, and make special trips out of them," she says. Sometimes she and Lisa fly their girls to meet them at doll events or to sculpting lessons with a doll artist. "We'll do mommy-daughter things like treating ourselves to manicures and pedicures." Marie explains. "Lisa also has a son who's around my sons' ages. We take our kids on trips and do fun things, so that our doll activities become special times with our children, too." Another favorite perk for her kids are the frequent trips to Disney theme parks where their mom premieres and signs many of her dolls.

Occasionally some of the other family members like to get in on the act and put in a guest appearance or two. (No surprise here as her family has done pretty well working as a group!) Marie's eighty-four-year-old father, for instance, has followed in Marie's sculpting steps. So far he has contributed two dolls to Marie's line—Georgette (1996) and Georgianna (1999)—and is currently working on a third. "My dad is awesome," she says with obvious pride. "He can draw anything. He has a very good eye, and really loves to sculpt. He has earned the title we lovingly gave him— 'Master Sculptor Osmond.'" His contributions mean the world to Marie, who likes to think of it as his lasting legacy to her doll line.

Mrs. Osmond may not sculpt, but she has surely made her mark in the doll world as well. "You know the Donny and Marie dolls that came out in the 1970s? Those were my

through the Osmond Family Fan Club. "Marie never did care for the doll's face too much, but she loved the idea," Mrs. Osmond recollects.

Best of all, Mrs. Osmond got her validation, and her husband got to eat humble pie—not to mention the doll! Marie laughs and explains, "After the very first modeling doll came out, they made a chocolate version of it, which my mother presented to my dad and said, 'Enjoy!'"

mother's idea. She was absolutely ahead of her time," Marie notes. "Now they do them all—NSync and other stars—but Mattel's Donny and Marie dolls were really one of the first on the market."

Even before she convinced Mattel to produce these dolls, Mrs. Osmond persuaded the company to create a Marie Osmond modeling doll, a thirty-inch doll that came with its own clothing patterns. Mattel officials didn't go for the concept at first, saying the dolls were too large. Mr. Osmond was less diplomatic in his veto. "When my mother came up with the idea of the modeling doll, my father thought she was nuts," Marie says. "'Nobody's going to buy a doll to sew clothes for,' he said, but my mom insisted that they would. My father told me, 'If that doll sells, I'll eat it.'" Mrs. Osmond would not give up on her idea, however, and everyone eventually relented.

Mattel agreed to make 1,000 dolls. The company even stamped a floral print one-piece bathing suit on the doll to satisfy Mrs. Osmond's concern for the doll's modesty when she discovered it wore no underclothes. They sold "like lightning," according to Mrs. Osmond, who offered them exclusively

12 *"I enjoyed this signing at Beachy's Doll House in Wauseon, Ohio. Edith and Daryl Beachy make doll collecting even more fun by dressing their daughter in the same costume as Peek-a-Boo. This is a living example of generations sharing the passion of doll collecting."*

13 *"You thought I was kidding! Here's proof of my broken toe at Lane's Toyland in Texarkana, Arkansas. I didn't let it stop me from enjoying the day—or Linda Varner's homemade chicken salad, which has become a tradition!"*

14 *"One of the main reasons I enjoy going to doll signings is to see some of my dear and avid doll collectors. Here are Betsy, Barb and Linda, who always treat me to their famous peanut butter and chocolate 'Buck-eyes!'"*

15 *"Two of my daughters, Jessica and Rachael, and Lisa's two daughters, Alexis and Tiffany, joined me for this signing at Enchanted Cottage in Provo, Utah, just minutes from my home."*

A PASSION FOR PERFECTION

For the most part, however, Lisa is Marie's most constant confederate in her doll enterprises. Lisa is the one who Marie calls at three in the morning with a great idea for a doll concept that has just struck her. "My reaction is 'write it down and call me tomorrow,'" Lisa jokingly groans.

"I can't help it, late night pizza really inspires me," Marie chimes in.

"Yeah, uh-huh," responds Lisa. "And when she's pregnant, look out!"

"Sometimes I think the folks at Knickerbocker are scared of me," Marie continues, with a mischievous giggle. "I typically come up with these ideas that throw them into a tizzy."

"A tizzy, yes, but a happy one!" insists Peggy Vicioso, the brand manager of Marie's doll line at Knickerbocker. "Marie's a kick to work with. She certainly keeps creative energies flowing. Her passion for this business is overflowing; it's impossible not to get excited about every new project when working with her. Marie is a sound businesswoman who understands the value of give-and-take. However, she will never compromise on quality."

"It's never easy working with someone who is demanding and strives for perfection, but Marie's 'tizzies' have led to some of her greatest dolls. And they are 'Marie Osmond' dolls, not 'Knickerbocker' dolls, so it is only right that she have a hands-on attitude," says Martin Krasner. "Marie is one of the most astute business people I have ever known. She has a vision of what her collection should be, and she knows how it should evolve. This strong sense of focus is an important element in the success of her collection. She is involved in each and every aspect, from the original concept down to the last shoe buckle. Regardless of whether she sculpts a doll herself or commissions another talented artist, she is equally involved in every detail. And she not only creates the dolls, but she directs every aspect of the marketing of her collection."

While it may vary from project to project, on most dolls Marie is closely involved in developing the creative concepts, choosing the sculptors, creating the themes, contributing ideas and direction, strategizing on marketing concepts and selling. "You name it," says Lisa, "she does it."

Karen Black, a longtime friend and neighbor of Marie, will be the first to tell you just how seriously Marie takes the smallest detail of her dolls. "She showed up at my house one day and said she was in a bind and could I help her on a dress she was working on. Now, I'm not a major seamstress or anything, but I said sure I'd be happy to help, thinking how hard could it be," Karen laughs. "Well, let me tell you, I was blown away. She was just so particular about everything! Every single thing had to be perfect and just so; I mean every little detail. It was so comical—it was this tiny piece that I thought I'd whip up in no time. No way! But you know what? It was an eye-opener to me

because I saw that it's not just throwing together a doll for her. It's a truly personal thing that really does reflect her, and so she is extremely meticulous." Apart from making her more cautious about accepting any last-minute sewing assignments, the experience has made Karen—a loyal collector of Marie's dolls—even more aware and appreciative of the tremen-

dous amount of attention that goes into each and every doll in Marie's line, particularly the smaller-sized ones.

"In addition to the fine quality sculpts, the hallmark to Marie's collection is its detailed costuming. Just when you think you have seen it all, there is always one more detail," notes Peggy Vicioso, adding that Marie's active hands-on working philosophy is a double-edged sword. "Her passion often requires us to jump through hoops," she good-naturedly bemoans. "Sometimes I think, 'We'll never get this executed in time,' then, through tireless persistence, we somehow are able to do it."

If Marie demands a lot of others, it's nothing to what she goes through herself. She is constantly thinking dolls, and scouting for talent and inspiration. Once during a concert performance, she spotted a cute baby girl in the audience. Marie was so drawn to her that she wanted to use her as a mini muse for one of her dolls. She invited the thrilled parents backstage and proceeded to take pictures of the little charmer. Usually, it's Marie who is posing for photos, but in this instance, she was the one taking all the shots of the adorable tot.

She is never too busy to spend time listening to her fans and collectors. "She has an amazing gracious patience with her public. I've attended doll events with her like the Doll and Teddy Bear Expo in Washington, D. C., and every five steps someone stops her to talk to her," says Karen Seamons, who helps create many costumes for Marie's dolls. "At that moment that person becomes the center of the universe for her, and she will stand and talk and not be rushed despite whatever else may be required of her. Believe me, I know her schedule. She is one busy lady! Yet that's secondary to Marie when there's someone who wants to have a moment of her time. She's very uplifting. I remember one particular gentleman who had been through a divorce; Marie was so sensitive in listening to him."

"She's always very cordial, sweet and accommodating, in fact maybe to a fault," says Karen Black. She has seen firsthand how Marie will put off dinner and rest after a show performance to meet with collectors who often have traveled long distances to see her show and have her sign their dolls. "She's just glad to do it," Karen says admiringly. "She takes a lot of pride in wanting people to feel happy with what she's done. It's her way of saying thank you. She's very appreciative of people liking what she does."

"I have seen her under all circumstances," insists doll artist and friend Beverly Stochr. "I kept waiting to see the other side. But there is no other side. That's her. I've seen her under a lot of stress and she doesn't let it get to her. She thinks of other people and keeps on going."

Karen Black enthusiastically seconds that: "She is a caring person who is very connected to real people and their real problems. She's never too busy to do the one-on-one things that mean the most. She's not just out for herself," Karen says. As an example of her friend's giving nature, she tells of Marie canceling some work commitments so that she could

16 *"Here is Peggy Vicioso, who heads our brand at L.L. Knickerbocker. In addition to being our brand manager, she is also the on-air host for Annette Funicello Bears. Peggy is a great asset to our team!"*

17 *"This is Marty Krasner, CEO of the L.L. Knickerbocker Company. In this picture, Marty's in seventh heaven with a comfortable chair, a computer with sales figures, and a telephone nearby. Isn't he too cute?"*

18 *"During our first trip to QVC-UK, we toured the famous Tower of London and stopped to take this picture. From left, we are: my manager, Karl Engemann, Lou Knickerbocker, me, an English Beefeater, my husband, Brian, and Lisa Hatch. This trip was too much fun!"*

18

spend the entire afternoon and night with Karen and her daughter, Mekel, who was getting married. Marie—who years earlier had created a doll named after Mekel, as well as one of Mekel's brother Cody—was not about to let the day pass without making it memorable. "She did my daughter's makeup, her nails and hair, and just made her feel like a queen. It was so fun. Marie was so busy, but she took the time. I'll never forget that and my daughter never will, either."

"I'm not afraid of hard work," Marie says. "My parents always instilled in us that you have to work hard to get what you want in life, but they also taught us that it should never be at the expense of human relationships, and that we should always make time for our family, friends and fans."

Fueled by this ingrained work ethic and a sensitivity to collectors' needs and wants, Marie unveiled her dolls in 1991. The Disney theme parks—so in keeping with her All-American image and the magic of childhood fantasy and ideals—were natural choices as premier venues.

"I've been associated with Disney since I can remember," Marie notes. "My brothers were discovered at Disneyland, and I've done various Disney anniversary celebrations, as well as broadcasts of the Children's Miracle Network Telethon from the theme parks. So Disney was a natural choice when I wanted to reach out to a broader retail audience for my dolls."

An equally perfect fit was her idea to simultaneously go on the QVC Network. As a child of television, she regarded the medium as the ideal forum for presenting her dolls to the public. As a businesswoman, she grasped the potential. "When I started out, I saw how it would greatly benefit retail doll stores to have the dolls receive television exposure. It would basically be free advertising for the retailers, and it would give them the chance to reach a new kind of collector. There are many different types of collectors and buyers. People who buy on QVC are definitely a different audience from those who buy in a store, on the internet, or through catalogs. Those who prefer buying in a store want to touch and feel the doll and fabrics, while those who buy over QVC don't feel the same need.

"I felt that, as a celebrity, I stood a good chance of reaching those television buyers on QVC. I also thought it was important that my fans be able to see that I knew what I was talking about; that I wasn't just another token celebrity endorsing a product, but that I had designed, created and, in some cases, sculpted the dolls. I think QVC was the right choice to establish and

help grow our brand for the first ten years, and we look forward to an even more rewarding relationship for many years to come. QVC enabled me to quickly show people that I was legitimate as a doll designer, sculptor and creator."

Marie—a "people person" if ever there was one—loved the sense of intimacy that QVC provided. "It's almost like a viewer having a one-on-one with the designer—it's the next best thing to being there" she says. "You hear the stories; you see the fabrics; you learn why the doll was created. It's like sitting with the artist in your own living room. Another great point is that with QVC, mothers, daughters and granddaughters can all sit in front of the TV and decide which dolls they're going to add to their collections and pass down from generation to generation."

"Marie loves good TV," says Lisa. "It's live and so you have to keep it fresh and come up with fun things." For Marie, that often involves put-

19

ting a personal twist on things. Nepotism and favoritism aren't dirty words in the Osmond camp. In fact, Marie loves nothing better than to be able to thrill family, friends and work colleagues with special surprises like naming dolls after them. Karen Seamons once mentioned in passing that a little doll that Marie had given her to costume resembled her granddaughter, Rylee. Marie agreed, and not only did she name the doll after Karen's granddaughter, but she also had a big blow-up done of a photo of the real Rylee. She then took both images of the darling toddler—the doll and the enlarged picture—on QVC, and the excited little toddler got her fifteen minutes of fame at the early age of three. Of course, grandma was as proud as she could be. She was also very appreciative. "I thought that was a really nice gesture on Marie's part," Karen says. "It's an example of how personal Marie will get every chance that she possibly can."

"In my job, it's not always easy to be on air for such a long time with someone," says QVC host Mary Beth Roe, "but it is with Marie. With her, there's always something going on. We have so much fun together—laughing and crying and carrying on. What makes us such a great team is that we both love dolls and we come to the show with similar interests. She does that with everyone. She tries to get on the same level with the person and find common interests."

19 *"I told you I was a collector first! Here I am at the 1998 Doll & Teddy Bear Expo East in Washington, D.C., having Robert Tonner sign my latest one-of-a-kind purchase of his. I admire his talent and sense of style."*

20 *"Here are Allen Finlinson, Karl Engemann and Lisa Hatch with me in the fall of 1993, the night of my last concert and just before I went into rehearsals for* The Sound of Music. *To date, these three have been with me for a total of sixty-three years. To be clear,* I *haven't been around that long!"*

highlights were Jessica's First Birthday, which was the second doll to be created and named after Marie's oldest daughter; the introduction of Rachael, named after Marie's second daughter; and Bryanna, which was the first in the Christmas series.

Innovation was the hallmark of 1993 with the premiere of the Greeting Card doll collection. The first of its kind on the market, it featured a 5½-inch doll nestled in a decorative greeting box that a collector could sign and mail in an accompanying envelope. "Although it's since been copied, at the time, it really was an out-of-the-box concept (no pun intended!) that no

numbers for her first all-Christmas show on QVC and, in June, for a live broadcast from Disneyland in Anaheim, California, where Marie simultaneously hosted the Children's Miracle Network Telethon.

Marie was developing a keen sense of what QVC collectors wanted, and she didn't hesitate to go to bat for concepts she truly believed in. For instance, she thought Beverly Stoehr's Rosie and Rags dolls—rag dolls done in porcelain—would be a big hit with viewers. But she initially had a difficult time getting QVC to accept the idea. The folks at QVC weren't sure collectors would like the dolls, since the concept was so different. Trusting Marie's judgement, QVC finally gave the dolls the nod and when they were aired, all 9,000 dolls sold out in twenty minutes. This was one of the first of many great hits in Marie's line. "I was so happy to be a part of this," Beverly says. "The response from the collectors was so great and the concept is still going strong, with new developments being incorporated into the line."

Marie—always the first to recognize the contributions of others to her line—graciously sent Beverly roses. "I still have them pressed in a book," says the artist, clearly touched by Marie's thoughtfulness.

one else had thought to do, and it did extremely well for us," says Lisa. The addition of new sculptors and designers such as Jan Hollebrands, Ann Jackson, Donna Stewart and Beverly Stoehr to the team also helped to keep the line fresh and varied as the company proudly introduced new series such as Storybook, Picture Day, Hat Box, Sweet Dreams, Fairy Tale and Petite Amour.

In 1994, Marie updated the Storybook concept by introducing adorable seven-inch dolls enclosed in artwork boxes featuring original poems from some of her favorite fairy tales and poems. Other popular pieces included Hareloom Bunny, Bunny Love, and Traci, a special edition Miracle Children doll that signs "I love you," again drawing on a theme close to her heart—the hearing-impaired.

By this time Marie and QVC were well on their way to forging a strong working relationship. Marie was fast becoming a regular draw for QVC's viewers, who tuned in in record

22 *"At a baby shower for my newborn son, Matthew, I posed with my dear friends, Gerri Engemann (Karl's wife), Kesti Poulsen and Breta Finlinson (Allen's wife). Not only are they real-live dolls, but they also served as inspirations for dolls I created and named after each of them."*

Taking On The Sculpting Challenge

Marie's sharp artistic eye continued to be refined. "As the line grew and people submitted doll heads, I would look at them, and I'd say, 'Well, yes, but we need the nose a little smaller and the eyes need to be larger, and maybe if you took some of the baby fat off of the cheeks,'" Marie says.

There was no question that, using her own taste as a collector, Marie could see what needed to be done, and how. It just remained to be seen whether she herself could actually execute her ideas into sculpted form. Always eager for a novel challenge, Marie decided to give sculpting a try. She sought instruction from noted doll artist and teacher Jack Johnston. "My first attempt at sculpting was in Cernit," she recalls. "I think one day I'll auction her off as a wicked witch; she was so ugly-looking!" After experimenting with Cernit for awhile, she found that while she liked working with the material, it was too labor- and time-intensive for making one face. It wasn't right for the needs of her doll line. Thinking she might have better luck with another medium, she decided to try clay. This time she turned to Beverly Stoehr for lessons.

Marie, who was touring with *The Sound of Music* at the time, invited Beverly to fly out for intensive training sessions at various cities along her performance route. During these sessions, which sometimes lasted from three to seven days at a stretch, Marie would work on the heads and faces in the mornings before a show. After each performance, she was back in the hotel room and back at the dollmaking lessons. Thanks to years of rehearsal practices, Marie was a quick study. "She would pick up things fast and she'd retain what I'd say," Beverly says. "But sculpting is not something that you do overnight; it's a craft, and you have to practice and build upon it. The more she did it, the more she understood. She's very receptive to learning, and she has her own ideas, which is good because that's how you develop your individuality."

Marie threw herself into the challenge with her customary drive. "Sometimes we'd work

23

until 3 a.m. She'd be all wound up after a performance, and come back at 10:30 or 11 p.m., and we'd sculpt until the early morning," Beverly recalls.

These marathon learning sessions were invaluable to Marie in many ways. She now had skills and a much better understanding of exactly what sculpting entailed. She also found it a lot of fun, and immensely therapeutic. "I absolutely adored learning to sculpt," Marie raves. "Working with Beverly is wonderful. She is so talented. We studied facial bone and muscle structure and experimented with a lot of techniques.

"I've worked so hard throughout my life that I've learned to play hard, too," she continues. "But it's the quiet moments that I enjoy the most. I really love my dolls. I love designing. I love sculpting. It's that quiet time that I think

---

23 *"Here I am with talented sculptor Beverly Stoehr in a hotel room in Houston, Texas, during my national tour of* The Sound of Music, *working on what would become my first sculpted porcelain doll, Olive May."*

Marie certainly had her hands full. In addition to her doll pursuits and actively mothering her, at the time, six kids, she was also busy on the television front. In 1998, she reunited with her brother Donny to star in the daytime entertainment talk show, *The Donny & Marie Show.* To commemorate this event, she created and debuted the Donny & Marie dolls in porcelain. Other 1998 debuts included Marie's successful Disney Babies series, with Baby Snow White being the first in the series and Baby Cinderella following shortly after.

Many exciting new series (some of them still among the most popular today) were unveiled in 1999—Tiny Tots, beginning with Olive May and Friends, debuted in January as the Today's Special Value (TSV) on QVC and sold out. The Tiny Tots are miniature versions of some of the most beloved dolls in Marie's line. The Wizard of Oz series debuted in February with Baby Dorothy, quickly followed by Baby Tin Man, Baby Scarecrow and Baby Cowardly Lion. The Wizard of Oz dolls were such hits that they were made into Tiny Tots soon after.

Not surprisingly, Marie has strong feelings about making dolls of high quality that are fun, playable and bring people together. "I've talked to a lot of women, and they say, 'We have dolls, but our daughters aren't really into collecting.' I strongly feel it's because the daughters never felt a connection," Marie insists. "They saw mommy's dolls sitting in a cupboard, but they never got to play with them or touch them. Don't put your dolls in a cabinet and let them sit there just to be dusted. Play with them! Some people are afraid because the dolls are made of porcelain. They shouldn't be. After all, porcelain is what children played with hundreds of years ago. And the porcelain that is used for producing my dolls is of the highest quality; it's not a flimsy porcelain that breaks when you breathe on it. So, play and have fun!

"I'm a collector, but I'm also a mother," Marie continues. "I felt there needed to be a 'bridge' doll, a collectible doll that younger girls can play with, through which they can learn to appreciate the beauty and value of dolls. If they become doll collectors, that's great! If they don't, that's okay, too. But almost every little girl, at some point, likes to play with dolls or at least has some interest in them. And if the moms are getting these great porcelain dolls—it was really just a natural progression."

Consequently, in 1999, Marie went after tomorrow's budding collectors with the introduction of Adora Belle ("why?...because she's adorable!" quips Marie) and Beauty Bug Ball vinyl toy dolls. That same year, the Adora Belle line was expanded to include reduced-size vinyl Belles with Cow Belle, Liberty Belle, Belle-E-Dancer and Cinder-Bella all being sold in shops. Another Adora Belle—Adora Belle Holiday Cheer—was designed to be sold exclusively in Target stores. The Beauty Bug Ball series was recreated in vinyl and sold on QVC. One especially noteworthy doll this year was Beary Best Friends, a collaboration with Boyds Bears.

The fact that the piece sold out quickly was the icing on the cake as far as Gary Lowenthal, the "Head Bean Hisself" at Boyds Bears, was concerned. What he really enjoyed was the opportunity to collaborate with Marie on the project. As Gary will—and does—readily admit in front of his wife, he's "smitten" with Marie and jumped at the chance to work with her. Jokingly, Gary goes on to relate that the depth of his infatuation extends even beyond his loyalty to their mutual QVC host, Mary Beth Roe. "Anyone who's ever watched me on QVC knows that I like to come on dressed as different characters. One time I came on dressed as a rock-n-roll type guy with my hair greased back and a cigarette pack rolled up in my sleeve. I had the make-up artist draw me a tattoo that said 'Mary Beth forever.' Marie came by later on while I was selling my TSV and she gave me a kiss. Well, the next time I came back, I'd crossed out Mary Beth's name and my tattoo now read 'Marie forever.' I guess I'm fickle," he chuckles unrepentantly. "I obviously like Marie very much. She's talented as an actress and singer, and, of course, she's beautiful. But what surprised me beyond her ability to design was how smart a business-woman she is, and how quick she is in under-standing certain marketing and merchandising concepts. If she wasn't so talented as an actress and singer, and didn't have such an upright and moral personality, she probably could have made a good theatrical agent.

"Sometimes Boyds Bears deals with people who ask us to do private label products for them, and they don't have any design input," Gary says, turning earnest. "Marie has a ton of design input in her dolls. I think that's very

important for people to know."

In 2000, the increasingly popular Tiny Tots got more company with the introduction of fif-teen new pieces to the series. August brought the sell-out of Helena on QVC. The entire edi-tion of 17,500 dolls sold out in less than two hours of on-air time. No doubt a part of the doll's appeal was that she was sculpted by internationally acclaimed doll artist Joke Grobben and came with an exclusive Christopher Radko ornament.

"I was thrilled to be a part of this," says Christopher. "Marie is a good saleswoman for both her dolls and my ornaments because her enthusiasm comes from her heart. She

loves sharing the joy of collecting and lifting people's spirits with what she does. That's also what I do with my ornaments; they bring smiles to people's faces."

"It's fun when you can share the passion," Marie agrees. "When I work on joint efforts with people like Christopher, Gary or Annette, I'm making a statement that we shouldn't be afraid of each other; we should work together instead. Gary worked with me because he wanted to introduce his bears to my doll collectors and I loved the idea of introducing my dolls to his bear customers. And that goes for everyone I've collaborated with. Christopher is so creative and has such energy that I feel a great synergy working together. I'm an avid collector of Christopher's art. I loved it when he would guest on *Donny & Marie* and share his ideas for the holidays. I was thrilled to collaborate with Christopher on Helena, the Today's Special Value on Collector's Day in August 2000."

"I think that Marie knew that my mother had been a great source of inspiration for me. So she offered to make a doll named after my mother, Helena. It was quite a wonderful doll, and so was the ornament that matched it," notes Christopher, who adds that Marie feels very much like a mem-ber of his family herself. "She is a fine human being. Over the years she has been through the mill. She's hardly had any time off for herself. I admire her spunk and her great moral strength."

Ironically, while Marie was getting accolades from her peers and her doll career continued on a steady ascendancy, in her personal life things were dramatically different. The difficult birth in July 1999 of her seventh child, Matthew, triggered a well-publicized bout of postpartum depression. As Marie describes it: "It's like your eyes are in

29 *"I'll never forget this day in May 1999 at the Mall of America, at Department 56, signing our exclusive pieces, the Marie Osmond Doll Museum (for their North Pole Village Collection) and Adora Belle North Pole. I was seven-and-a-half months pregnant, and I was ready to kill my manager, Karl, for booking this signing so close to my delivery date!"*

30 *"I am such a fan and an avid collector of Christopher Radko's ornaments, and I've been lucky enough to work with him on several occasions. Here we are on the set of QVC with our collaborative Jingle Belle Radko ornament."*

31 *"Here I'm grinning and 'bearing' it with the Head Bean Hisself, Gary Lowenthal, as we hold Beary Best Friends on the QVC set. Things are never boring at QVC when Gary's around."*

the back of your head, and you just want to close them and never open them. You're incredibly tired. Not only do you have a new baby to take care of, but, you know, I have six other children as well."

Happily, Marie is doing better these days, and she is adamant about encouraging others going through the same difficulties. She feels so strongly about getting her message out that she wrote a book entitled *Behind the Smile* (Warner Books, May 2001). "Even though I believe I'm through the worst of it, I still have some bad days. But it doesn't scare me anymore," says Marie. "These days, women want it all—a family and a career—but speaking for myself, it would be impossible without a higher source in my life. Religion isn't supposed to make you weird, you know. It's like a fourth leg on a chair—it helps keep you balanced and should give you a proper perspective about what's really important. I've studied many religions, and I know I've found a wholeness in mine."

When asked whether dolls serve as a source of strength and support, Marie—with her inherent optimism once more firmly in place—deflects the bad, preferring to focus on the positive. "I don't think collecting relates to personal problems. I do know dolls bring joy. I think doll collecting is fun and nurturing, and something that we collectors love having in our lives because it's sometimes how we find our childhood and love ourselves a little, too."

32

"She's worked a lot, and she did not have much time to play. She probably missed out on some childhood experiences," Marie's mother concedes, "but she's certainly making up for lost time now with her dolls. She's always excited. Life has meant so much to her. She's just made the most of it, I think."

"It appears to me that the most important things in Marie's life are her family and her faith," notes Peggy Vicioso, who has known and worked with Marie for eight years. "She is also very human, and I think her fans can relate to her as if she were their friend or neighbor. Her openness about any personal struggles has made her even closer to her fans."

"She doesn't hesitate talking to collectors about the challenges she faces," Lisa notes. "I've seen her break into tears many times at signings when collectors share their own life experiences with Marie. They break down and hug each other and cry. Marie thrives on that personal connection with her collectors."

"I love doll lovers," Marie exclaims. "They are sweet, sweet people. I love hearing personal stories about their lives and how certain dolls hold special meaning for them. That's the payoff for me! That's what collecting is all about.

"I have received hundreds of letters, many of them very moving, about the dolls and what they mean in people's lives," Marie says. "The feelings associated with them are timeless and invaluable." Few letters have moved her as deeply as one from a mother who wrote about her terminally ill daughter. The little girl, whose name was Jessica, had never been a doll collector. In fact, she was a bit of a tomboy. But she fell in love with Marie's Jessica doll, which was named after Marie's second daughter, who is also a tomboy.

"Jessica, who was about five years old, had terminal bone cancer. Her mom wrote me a letter saying, 'I want you to know that you do more than design dolls.' She explained that as her daughter went through chemotherapy and other types of treatment procedures, it was very difficult for her to be held or touched because it hurt her so much. But she never wanted her mother to know how bad the pain was. So, instead she would say, 'My doll Jessica doesn't want to be touched tonight; she's hurting.' And then her mom would know how she was feeling. Or she'd say something like, 'Jessica's legs really ache, and I need to rub them for her,' which would clue her mother that the real Jessica needed a leg rub herself."

The mother ended her letter by telling Marie that her little girl had passed away and that she'd been buried with her beloved doll. She also expressed her entire family's heartfelt thanks and gratitude—they all loved Marie because it was through her doll that they had been able to communicate better with their beloved Jessica and ease her pain. The mother went on to say, "You do more than design dolls; you create lifetime memories."

"This story tells you that dolls are more than just dolls, and they need to be more. You might ask why I do this—why I'm involved. It's because of people like this," Marie says simply.

32 *"In between shows in the Green Room at QVC, I put the final make-up touches on the prototype of what would become Adora Belle Holiday 1999 with a little help from my newborn son, Matthew."*

A New Decade Brings New Ambitions

Heartened by a renewed sense of purpose and a strong support system of family, faith, friends and fans, Marie is back in full force. She has thrown herself into making 2001—her line's tenth anniversary—truly memorable. And there's a lot to be hopeful and proud of, including some curious reversals. For instance, Marie gets a kick out of seeing the evolution of support, especially among retailers, of her line. Ten years ago, Marie's dolls were not embraced by a large segment of the retail doll industry, which, up until the past few years, feared that electronic retailing would compete for the same customer. Now it's completely flip-flopped. "Today," Marie states, "we've proven that retail stores reap the benefits."

"We love the spin-off from QVC," says Sue Rogers of Lane's Toyland. "It reaches out to a broader range of collectors, and it has attracted new types of customers into our shop."

"Marie is one of the best things the doll industry has going for it. I think it's wonderful that she sells her dolls on QVC," says Jackie Landreth, owner of the Greensboro, North Carolina-based The Doll Market, the largest doll shop in the United States. "It gives dolls and the doll community lots of exposure, and attracts new customers. Her celebrity status, her talents as a doll designer and the dolls in her line all add up to more attention and awareness for all of us. Whenever she airs on QVC, our store's sales usually go up."

Today, QVC enjoys a strong presence in the world of collectible dolls, and Marie's line represents one of the steadiest and most significant audience draws in the category. Marie's appeal is undeniable, and a definite collector draw, according to Mary Beth Roe. "Over the years, people have totally fallen in love with her. She's wonderful, warm, friendly, kind, witty, funny, and you can tell she cares what people think. People love seeing her on QVC. It's all-live, and her fans can call in and interact with her. I think it's their love of her that draws them to the show. Then while they're watching, they start to fall in love with the dolls for whatever reason—whether it's sentimental, triggered by a name or a look. Or maybe it's a beautiful dress or face that captures their attention. And there's a trust factor, too. They know and believe her. Her enthusiasm gets a lot of people to begin collecting her dolls who might never have started if it hadn't been for Marie."

One of Marie's favorite ways to get feed-back from collectors is through her doll website (www.osmond.com/marie/dolls). "Collectors have come to know and love Kesti Poulsen, in my office, as she facilitates our site and communicates back and forth with them on my behalf. I

33 *"Sonja Bryer and I, in her sculpting studio, used calipers to measure the clay head of what was to become Remember Me—the doll I'm holding on the cover of this book!"*

34 *"Measuring my head after a week of intense sculpting, I found it had shrunk! Sonja and I had too much fun that week!"*

was a mouth, laughing at me, as if to say, 'It's never gonna happen. Give it up, Marie.' Inside I was shouting, 'Why, why, why do I get myself into these things?'"

It was too late for regrets. Time was ticking and she had a lot of work ahead of her. It was slow and difficult at first, but they kept at it. With Sonja and Lisa working alongside her, Marie labored for four days, typically going for seven hours straight with only an occasional snack break. "The first couple of days were rather intense and stressed because of the time crunch to finish the doll," Sonja admits. "But we did manage to have fun, especially the last couple of days when we saw things were coming together."

As Marie relaxed and gained more confidence, a vision for the doll began to materialize. Sonja saw a new side to Marie, as well. "When I first met Marie I noticed that she was so friendly with everyone," she says. "When we started the classes, I came to see that she's also a very strong woman who knows what she wants.

"At first, I didn't like that she wasn't taking my instructions. Lisa joked about it, saying we were like yin and yang. 'Sonja tells you to take the clay off and you put it back on,' she'd say to Marie. Then I realized it was because Marie had her own ideas of how she wanted it to look, which is good for an artist. It shows she has her own sense of creativity, and that's what makes the doll her doll. I really liked that…after I thought about it a little," Sonja says with a rueful laugh.

"She did a really good job," Sonja concedes. "When she started sculpting I saw that she was a much better sculptor than I had realized. I found out that she is really talented."

Marie has no pretensions about being a great sculptor, however. Looking into the future, she defines her role in the industry as more of a goodwill ambassador for doll artists. "I'm an okay sculptor—and I feel I've gotten better—but I don't think I'm the most talented doll artist out there. I don't want to inundate the collections with just my sculpts. One of my goals in our doll

39 "*We celebrated Karl's seventieth birthday backstage in the Green Room with (from left), Lisa, Marie D'Amore holding my one-month-old son Matthew, Tammy Knickerbocker, me and the birthday boy. (As you can see, Lisa and I never graduated from the 'bunny ears' stage!)*"

brand is to reach a new audience. What I do is try to educate people by saying, 'Look! Isn't this a great face? This is what makes it unique…this is what makes it special. This is by Sonja Bryer. This is by Beverly Stoehr.' 'This is a Joke Grobben,' etc.

"I'm honored and thrilled when doll artists agree to work with me. There are a lot of wonderful new sculptors out there who will never be recognized unless someone gives them a shot. I try to help my collectors become aware of other artists. Most people can't afford a $5,000, one-of-a-kind or limited-edition doll, so I introduce them to these fabulous artists through my line by producing their sculpts at an affordable price. This creates great synergy with artists and collectors," says Marie, noting that she often hears from people who began collecting dolls by certain artists from her line and then went on to purchase limited editions produced by those artists themselves.

It's not just high-sounding talk, either. Marie's putting her company's doll line where her sentiments are. For example, as part of its tenth anniversary, Marie's line will be presenting special limited editions of ten by noted artists. "When we offered ten dolls, at $1,500 each, by Carole Bowling they sold out the night before we even went on air. And now Carole has said she'd love to do another doll with us because I promoted Carole Bowling, not Marie Osmond.

"This is a fabulous industry filled with so much talent. When talented people get around other talented people, there's just great energy that will be created, if you let it," Marie insists. "We can and should help one another."

Marie's strong sense of loyal solidarity defines her, as it defines her doll line and her commitment to the people, passions and principles that mean the most to her. Sentiment and personal ties—combined with Marie's charisma—all play vital roles in the popularity and commercial success of Marie's dolls. Yet, the roots of this success are much deeper. Starting from childhood, when she first hugged little Bubbles to her chest (a doll she still has to this day) through many cherished associations, Marie has spent a lifetime interweaving memories, allegiances and bonds of affection that foster creativity and commitment in herself and others. This "All-American icon," loved and admired by thousands, returns the gift. She, and her dolls, bring happiness and comfort into people's lives. Whether inspired by Marie or moved by a particular doll, people want to share her passions and dream her dreams. And as she faces the future, Marie smiles, holds out her hand and welcomes everyone to share the journey.

The Collection

The dolls produced by the Marie Osmond Fine Porcelain Collector Doll Line are presented on the following pages, in alphabetical order, by series. Special Editions, and dolls that are new in 2001, are at the end of the section. To quickly find the doll you are seeking, please consult the index on page 159.

RIGHT:
Wedding Belle, *vinyl, 15 inches, sculpted by Marie Osmond, hand-numbered edition, 2000*

BELOW, FROM LEFT:
Adora Beau, *porcelain, 14 inches, edition of 2000, 1999;* **Adora Belle Toy Fair,** *porcelain, 9 inches, edition of 500, 1999;* **Adora Belle,** *porcelain, 14 inches, edition of 20,000, 1997;* **Wedding Belle,** *vinyl, 15 inches, hand-numbered edition, 2000. All dolls are sculpted by Marie Osmond.*

ABOVE, BACK ROW, FROM LEFT:
Adora Belle Holiday 1999, *vinyl, 15 inches, open edition;* **Adora Belle Holiday 2000**, *vinyl, 16 inches, open edition;* **Adora Belle Holiday Cheer**, *vinyl, 14 inches, Target exclusive, open edition, 1999;* **Adora Belle North Pole**, *porcelain, 14 inches, Department 56 exclusive, edition of 1,000, 1999*

FRONT ROW, FROM LEFT:
Jingle Belle, *porcelain, 14 inches, edition of 10,000, 1997;* **Adora Belle Night Before Christmas**, *porcelain, 14 inches, edition of 7,500, 1998. All dolls are sculpted by Marie Osmond.*

Jessica's Daddy Daughter Date,
*porcelain, 28 inches, co-sculpted
by Marie Osmond and Beverly
Stoehr, edition of 5,000, 1997*

FROM LEFT:
Count Cocky Cockroach, *1998;* **Madame Butterfly,**
1997; **Queen Bee,** *1996;* **Lady Bug,** *1996;* **Countess
Caterpillar,** *1998. All dolls are porcelain, 9½ inches,
sculpted by Linda Henry in editions of 7,500 each.*

FROM LEFT:
Baron Von Beetle, *1998;* **Miss Quito,** *2000;*
Damsel Dragonfly, *1996;* **Sir Stink Bug,** *1997;*
Baroness Beetle, *1998. All dolls are porcelain,*
9½ inches, sculpted by Linda Henry in edi-
tions of 7,500 each. The series was retired
after the introduction of Miss Quito.

LEFT:
Queen Bee, *porcelain,*
9½ inches, sculpted by Linda
Henry, edition of 7,500, 1996.

FROM LEFT:
Erin, *22 inches, sculpted by Maryse Nicole, edition of 2,500, 1992;* **Chrissy**, *21 inches, sculpted by Margaret Yokee, edition of 5,000, 1996;* **Amy**, *22 inches, sculpted by Linda Henry, edition of 2,300, 1991;* **Michael**, *22 inches, sculpted by Linda Henry, edition of 2,500, 1991. All dolls are porcelain.*

FROM LEFT:
Georgia, *20 inches, sculpted by Maryse Nicole, edition of 2,500, 1992;* **Hillary,** *20 inches, sculpted by Maryse Nicole, edition of 2,500, 1992;* **Bunny Blues,** *17 inches, sculpted by Sonja Bryer, edition of 5,000, 1998. All dolls are porcelain.*

BIT-O-BUNNY Series

FROM LEFT:
Lovely Lilac; Snowball; Cranbunny; Just Peachy; Mint Patty. *All dolls have mohair plush bodies by Lisa Applebeary and porcelain faces sculpted by Marie Osmond. They are each 4½ inches high, open editions introduced in 1999.*

Story Book Cassette Collection,
narrated by Marie Osmond and
Mike Wuergler, 1995

Spring, *porcelain, 24 inches, sculpted by Jerri Mowry, edition of 5,000, 1995*

Chenoa, *porcelain, 16 inches, sculpted by Denise Krause, edition of 2,500, 1998*

BACK ROW, FROM LEFT:
Maria (Spanish), *17 inches, sculpted by Vincent De Filippo, 1991;* **Cindy (Afro-American),** *18 inches, sculpted by Vincent De Filippo, 1991;* **Bonnie Jean (Scottish),** *17 inches, sculpted by Jerri Mowry, 1995;* **Usha (Indian),** *17 inches, sculpted by Jerri Mowry, 1995*

FRONT ROW, FROM LEFT:
Tonika (Eskimo), *18 inches, sculpted by Jerri Mowry, 1994;* **Li-Chyn (Oriental),** *17 inches, sculpted by Vincent De Filippo, 1991;* **Chenoa (Indian),** *16 inches, sculpted by Denise Krause, 1998. All dolls are porcelain editions of 2,500 each.*

CHRISTMAS
Series

FROM LEFT:
Holly, *porcelain, musical bean bag, 13 inches, Grump reproduction, edition of 2,500, 1993;* **Father Christmas 1994,** *porcelain, 21 inches, sculpted by Jeanette Arnett, edition of 1,000*

Christmas 1994

53

FROM LEFT:
Bryanna 1992, *edition of 1,000; (seated)* **Bryanna 1994**, *edition of 7,500;* **Bryanna 1995**, *edition of 3,500. All dolls are porcelain, 17 inches, and sculpted by Rita Schmidt.*

SARAFINA SNOWFLAKE, *porce-lain, 15 inches, sculpted by Cindy Shafer, edition of 11,000, 1996*

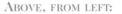

ABOVE, FROM LEFT:
Tree Top Angel 1995, *porcelain, 18 inches, sculpted by Beverly Stoehr, edition of 2,500;* **Tree Top Angel 1999,** *porcelain, 14 inches, sculpted by Cindy Shafer, edition of 2,500*

RIGHT, FROM LEFT:
Olive May Christmas Radko Ornament, *glass, 7 inches, edition size not available, 1999;* **Adora Belle Radko Ornament,** *glass, 6 inches, open edition, 1998;* *(on tree)* **Mini Jingles & Belle Ornaments,** *from top of tree moving down:* **Mini Jingles Country (boy),** *4 inches, sculpted by Beverly Stoehr, edition of 2,500, 1998;* **Mrs. Claus and Santa,** *4 inches, sculpted by Beverly Stoehr, edition of 2,500, 1998;* **Mini Jingles & Belle,** *4 inches, sculpted by Beverly Stoehr, edition of 2,500, 1996;* **Mini Jingles Country (girl),** *4 inches, sculpted by Beverly Stoehr, edition of 2,500, 1998;* **Mini Jingles & Belle as Mickey & Minnie,** *4 inches, sculpted by Beverly Stoehr, exclusive Disney edition of 1,000, 1998*

ABOVE:
Kimberly, *porcelain, 20 inches,
sculpted by Beverly Stoehr, edition
of 1,000, 1997*

FROM LEFT:
Constance, *20 inches, Bru reproduction, edition of 500, 1997; Catherine, 21 inches, A. Marque repro-*
duction, edition of 500, 1991; Christine, 19 inches, Jumeau reproduction, edition of 500, 1991; (seated)
Marisa, *22 inches, Jumeau reproduction, edition of 250, 1991. All dolls are porcelain.*

Victoria, *porcelain, 21 inches, Bru reproduction, edition of 500, 1991*

FROM LEFT:
Anna, *porcelain, 22 inches, Kestner reproduction, edition of 250, 1991;* **Audrey,** *porcelain, 21½ inches, Jumeau reproduction, edition of 500, 1997;* **Grandma Kit,** *porcelain head and limbs, composition body, 30 inches, Wolfie reproduction, edition of 500, 1995*

FROM LEFT:
(seated) Lauren, 19 inches, Bru reproduction, edition of 500, 1995; Crystal, 23 inches, Mein Liebling reproduction, edition of 250, 1991; Alesia, 21 inches, Bru reproduction, edition of 250, 1993. All dolls are porcelain.

FROM LEFT:
Sitting Pretty, *porcelain, 16½ inches, sculpted by Juanita Openshaw, edition of 1,500, 1999;* **Baby Marie Collector's Club**, *vinyl, 19½ inches; sculpted by Beverly Stoehr, edition of 100, 1998;* **Baby Marie Nighttime**, *vinyl, 19½ inches, sculpted by Beverly Stoehr, edition of 200, 1998;* **Faith**, *porcelain, 13½ inches, sculpted by Cindy Shafer, edition of 2,500, 1996*

FROM LEFT:
Morgan 1997; Morgan 1995; Morgan 1996. *All dolls are porcelain, 17 inches, Mein Leibling reproductions, editions of 1,500 each.*

TOP, FROM LEFT:
Angelic & Sweetness, *porcelain bookends, 6 inches, sculpted by Sonja Bryer, numbered edition, 1998;* **Watch Case Doll,** *1¾ inches, Kewpie reproduction, sculpted by Beverly Stoehr, open edition, 1995;* **First Kiss,** *boy and girl vignette, 8 inches, Pucker Up reproduction, edition of 2,500, 1995*

ABOVE, FROM LEFT:
Bunny Love 1998, *edition of 2,500;* **Bunny Love 1995,** *edition of 8,000;* **Bunny Love 1994,** *edition of 2,500;* **Bunny Love Cherub,** *edition of 5,000, 1996;* **Some Bunny Loves You,** *edition of 2,500, 1995;* **Bunny Love Christmas,** *edition of 2,500, 1994;* **Bunny Love Angel,** *edition of 2,500, 1996. All dolls are porcelain Bunny Love reproductions and 6 inches.*

FROM LEFT:
Tush, *8 inches, Dionne Quintuplets reproduction, 1994;* **Sophia,** *in wicker basinette, 7 inches, Robie reproduction, 1995;* **Angela,** *15 inches, Bru reproduction, 1996. All dolls are porcelain editions of 2,500 each.*

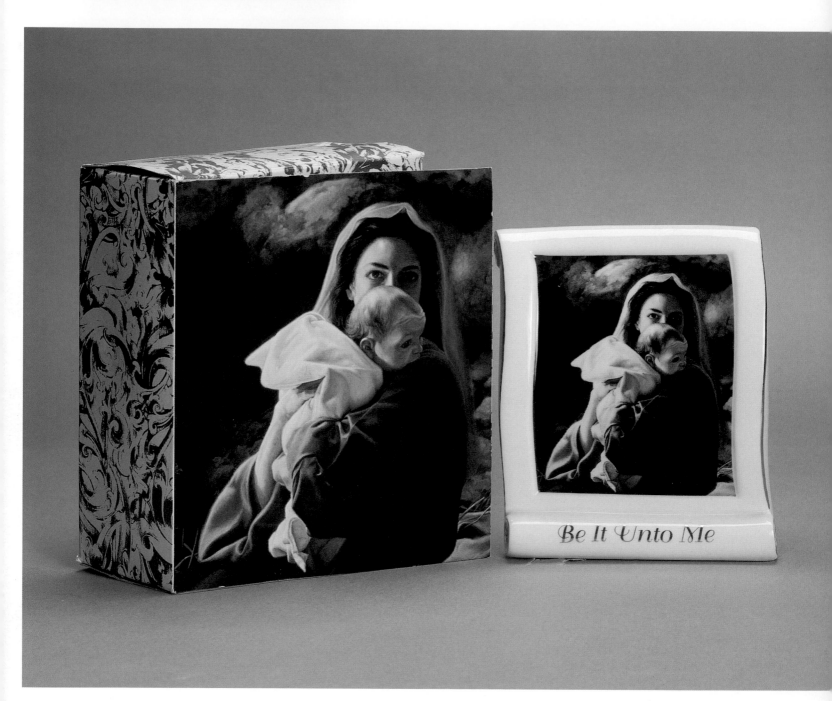

Be It Unto Me, *greeting box with porcelain scroll inside, 4½ inches x 5½ inches, artwork of Liz Lemon Swindle, hand-numbered edition, 2000*

FROM LEFT:
(seated) **Cissy**, *16 inches, sculpted by Cindy Shafer, edition of 2,500, 1996;* **Sarah**, *18 inches, sculpted by Maryse Nicole, edition of 2,500, 1992;* **Sarita**, *18 inches, sculpted by Maryse Nicole, edition of 2,500, 1992;* **Kylee**, *14 inches, sculpted by Charlotte Bellsmith, edition size and year of introduction unknown; (seated)* **Hallie**, *14 inches, sculpted by Ann Jackson, edition size, and year of introduction unknown. All dolls are porcelain.*

DEAR TO MY HEART
Series

Georgianna,
porcelain, 20 inches,
sculpted by
George Osmond,
edition of 1,500, 1999

LEFT, FROM LEFT:
Tammy, *sculpted by Maryse Nicole, 1992;* **Breta,** *sculpted by Maryse Nicole, 1992;* **Gerri,** *sculpted by Maryse Nicole, 1992;* **Patricia,** *sculpted by Vincent De Filippo, 1991;* **Lisa,** *sculpted by Vincent De Filippo, 1991. All dolls are 17 inches high and porcelain editions of 2,500 each.*

LEFT, BACK ROW, FROM LEFT:
Alexis Christmas, *18 inches, sculpted by Lisa Hatch, edition of 2,500, 1997;* **Tiffy,** *19 inches, sculpted by Lisa Hatch, edition of 1,500, 1998;* **Georgette,** *19 inches, sculpted by George Osmond, edition of 2,500, 1996.*
FRONT ROW, FROM LEFT:
Karen, *17 inches, sculpted by Rita Schmidt, edition of 2,500, 1996;* **Ozeanna,** *17 inches, sculpted by Charlotte Bellsmith, edition of 2,500, 1992. All dolls are porcelain.*

Garden Angel, *porcelain,*
12 inches, sculpted by
Kathleen Fitzpatrick,
edition of 2,500, 1998

EXPRESSIONS OF LOVE Series

TOP:
Puppy Love, *porcelain, 14 inches, sculpted by Beverly Stoehr, edition of 5,000, 2000*

ABOVE, FROM LEFT:
I Love You Beary Much, *23 inches, sculpted by Marie Osmond, bear by Annette Funicello, edition of 20,000, 1996;* **Bee Mine**, *20 inches, sculpted by Beverly Stoehr, edition of 5,000, 2000;* **I'll Love You Til The Cows Come Home**, *22 inches, sculpted by Rita Schmidt, edition of 5,000; 1998. All dolls are porcelain; animals are plush.*

Cinderella Princess, *porcelain,*
18 inches, sculpted by Sandra Bilotto,
Disney exclusive edition of 250, 1999

RIGHT, FROM LEFT:
Rapunzel, *19½ inches, sculpted by Jerri Mowry;* **Cinderella**, *22 inches, sculpted by Lisa Hatch; (foreground)* **Shelby**, *24 inches long, sculpted by Cindy Shafer. All dolls are porcelain editions of 5,000 each, introduced in 1996.*

BELOW, FROM LEFT:
Alice in Wonderland, *18 inches, sculpted by Juanita Openshaw, 1994;* **Snow White**, *19 inches, sculpted by Beverly Stoehr, 1993;* **Sleeping Beauty**, *18½ inches, sculpted by Marie Osmond, 1997;* **Little Red Riding Hood**, *17 inches, sculpted by Linda Henry, 1994. All dolls are porcelain editions of 5,000 each.*

Gene, *porcelain, 27½ inches,*
sculpted by Cindy Shafer, edition
of 2,500, 1995

From left:
Sunflower, 1996; Pansy, 1997; Poinsettia, 1995. All dolls are Cupid reproductions in porcelain editions of 3,000 each and 5½ inches.

FOUR SEASONS
Series

BACK ROW, FROM LEFT:
April, *1991;* **Joy,** *1992.*
FRONT ROW, FROM LEFT:
Summer, *1991.* **Amber,** *1993. All dolls are porcelain editions of 2,500 each, 24 inches and sculpted by Vincent De Filippo.*

FROM LEFT:
Alexandra, porcelain, 16½ inches, sculpted by Linda Henry, edition of 1,500, 1996; Tatiana, porcelain, 16½ inches, sculpted by Linda Henry, edition of 1,500, 1995

85

"FALLEN LEAVES"

FROM LEFT:
Fallen Leaves, *8 inches, 1995;* **Winter Wonder**, *7 inches, 1995;*
Spring Showers, *7 inches, 1994;* **Summer Days**, *7 inches, 1995.*
*All dolls are porcelain Heubach reproductions, sculpted by
Donna Stewart in editions of 4,000 each.*

TOP, FROM LEFT:
Mother's Day annual editions: 1997, *sculpted by Beverly Stoehr;* **1999,** *sculpted by Sonja Bryer;* **1998,** *sculpted by Margie Costa;* **1996,** *sculpted by Marie Osmond;* **1993,** *Jumeau reproduction. All dolls are porcelain and 5½ inches. (Not shown: 1994; 1995.)*

ABOVE, FROM LEFT:
Christmas annual editions: 1995, *Dulce reproduction;* **1994,** *K. Princess reproduction;* **1997,** *sculpted by Beverly Stoehr;* **1998,** *sculpted by Margie Costa;* **1996,** *sculpted by Marie Osmond;* **1993,** *Jumeau reproduction. All dolls are porcelain and 5½ inches.*

Virginia Marie, *porcelain,*
6 inches, Jumeau reproduction,
edition of 3,000, 1993

Haute Half Doll, *porcelain, 8 inches, sculpted by Michael Everet, hand-numbered edition, 2000*

I CAN DREAM
Series

*(seated) **Dottie**, 11 inches, sculpted by Vincent De Filippo, edition of 5,000, 1992; **Marta**, 10 inches, sculpted by Marie Osmond, edition of 5,000, 1996; **Bubbles**, 11 inches, sculpted by Lisa Hatch, edition of 300, 1997; **Chelsea**, 11 inches, sculpted by Vincent De Filippo, edition of 5,000, 1992; (seated) **Trina**, from Trina & Tracy—Sisterly Love set, porcelain, 9½ inches, sculpted by Maryse Nicole, Disney exclusive edition of 250, 1992; (in wagon) **Macie**, 11 inches, sculpted by Vincent De Filippo, edition of 5,000, 1993. All dolls are porcelain.*

BACK ROW, FROM LEFT:
Savannah, *sculpted by Vincent De Filippo, 1993;* **Carrie,** *sculpted by Lisa Hatch, 1997;* **Beth,** *sculpted by Vincent De Filippo, 1991.*
FRONT ROW, SEATED, FROM LEFT:
McKensie, *Pouty reproduction, sculpted by Maryse Nicole, 1992;* **Jennifer,** *sculpted by Vincent De Filippo, 1991;* **Dottie Anne,** *sculpted by Sandra Bilotto, 1998. All dolls are porcelain editions of 5,000 each and 11 inches.*

JESSICA'S BEST FRIENDS Series

Dance Company, *porcelain,
5½ inches, sculpted by
Alex Liao, numbered edition, 1999*

Romeo & Juliet, *porcelain,*
7 inches, A. Marque reproduc-
tion, edition of 1,500, 1999

MAGIC OF CHRISTMAS *Series*

FOREGROUND:

Stopping for Christmas, *ornament, 3½ inches;* Santa's Workshop Snow Globe *(Christmas series), 5 inches, hand-numbered edition, 1999;* Under the Mistletoe, *ornament, 3½ inches;* Memories of Christmas Snow Globe *(Christmas series), 7½ inches, hand-numbered edition, 1998;* Tree Topper *ornament, 4 inches.*

ON TREE, CLOCKWISE FROM BOTTOM LEFT:

Sleep Tight, *ornament, 3 inches;* Picture Perfect, *ornament, 3½ inches;* Yummy for his Tummy, *ornament, 3 inches. All ornaments are resin, sculpted by Alex Laio and introduced in 1999.*

MIRACLE CHILDREN Series

RIGHT, FROM LEFT:
Becky, *Twirp reproduction, 1994;* Pierre, *Pouty reproduction, 1992;* Annie, *Googly reproduction, 1993;* Caitlin & Bently, *Bru reproduction, 1994;* Mekel, *Twirp reproduction, 1993. All dolls are porcelain annual editions and 9½ inches.*

ABOVE, FROM LEFT:
(behind bed) **Tina**, *Twirp reproduction, 1994;* (on bed) **Bessie Bathtime**, *A. Marque reproduction, 1998;* (seated) **Flora**, *Bru reproduction, 1993;* **Katie**, *Hilda reproduction, 1991;* **Celeste**, *A. Marque reproduction, 1994;* (seated) **Marilyn**, *Hilda reproduction, 1992. All dolls are porcelain annual editions and 9 ½ inches.*

ABOVE:
Traci, *porcelain, 11 inches, sculpted by Linda Henry and Margaret Yokee, edition of 20,000, 1994*

ABOVE, SEATED, FROM LEFT:
Stephanie, 9½ inches, *Hilda reproduction, 1991;* **Cody,** *9½ inches, Bruno reproduction, 1993;* **Shannon,** *9½ inches, Hilda reproduction, 1992*
STANDING, FROM LEFT:
Courtnie, *9½ inches, Hilda reproduction, 1992;* **Denise,** *9½ inches, A. Marque reproduction, 1996;* **Gina, 11 inches, Googly reproduction, 1992. All dolls are porcelain annual editions.*

ABOVE, FROM LEFT:
(seated) **Betty,** *Pouty reproduction, 1992;* **Faith,** *Hilda reproduction, 1993;* **Ginger,** *Googly reproduction, 1997;* (seated) **Frenda,** *Hilda reproduction, 1992. All dolls are porcelain annual editions and 9½ inches.*

LEFT, FROM LEFT:
Melinda, *A. Marque reproduction, 1991;* **Aaron,** *Kammer & Reinhardt reproduction, 1993;* **Heather,** *Pouty reproduction, 1991. All dolls are porcelain annual editions and 9½ inches.*

BELOW, CLOCKWISE, FROM LEFT:
Linda, *sculpted by Maryse Nicole, 1992;* **Elizabeth,** *Hilda reproduction, 1991;* **Cherish,** *Pouty reproduction, 1992;* **Danielle,** *sculpted by Maryse Nicole, 1992;* **Melissa,** *Hilda reproduction, 1991;* (seated) **Shawn,** *Pouty reproduction, 1992. All dolls are porcelain annual editions and 9½ inches.*

ABOVE, FROM LEFT:
Tiffany, 9½ inches, *Pouty reproduction, 1991;* **Rebecca,** 9½ inches, *A. Marque reproduction, 1991;* **Gabriela,** 11 inches, *sculpted by Vincent De Filippo, 1992. All dolls are porcelain annual editions.*

LEFT:
Miracle Rosie & Rags, *porcelain, 11 inches, sculpted by Beverly Stoehr, edition of 20,000, 1996*

LEFT:
Baby Miracles, *porcelain, 18 inches, sculpted by Sonja Bryer, edition of 5,000, 1998*

BELOW, FROM LEFT:
Lindsay, *porcelain, 11 inches, sculpted by Maryse Nicole, edition of 300, 1992;* **Lindsay I Peeked**, *porcelain, 11 inches, sculpted by Maryse Nicole, edition of 500, year of introduction unknown.*

FROM LEFT:
(seated) Motherly Love, *14 inches, sculpted by Sonja Bryer, edition of 2,500, 1998;* Virginia & Jordan, *20 inches, Mein Leibling reproduction, edition of 3,000, 1994;* From God's Arms, *17 inches, sculpted by Marie Osmond, edition of 5,000, 1997. All dolls are porcelain.*

Emily, *porcelain, 17 inches,*
sculpted by Maryse Nicole, edition
of 2,500, 1992

The dolls on these pages do not belong to any particular series.

ABOVE:
Amy Kathlyn, *porcelain, 22 inches, sculpted by Rita Schmidt, edition of 5,000, 1996*

ABOVE RIGHT:
Rachelle, *porcelain, 22 inches, sculpted by Marie Osmond, edition of 1,500, 1997*

RIGHT:
Caterpillars to Butterflies, *porcelain, 12 inches, sculpted by Sonja Bryer, annual edition, 1999*

QUITE A PAIR
Series

Elise, porcelain, 32 inches,
sculpted by Lisa Hatch, edition
of 2,500, 1997

RIGHT, FROM LEFT:

Raimi, *28 inches, sculpted by Margie Costa, edition of 2,500, 1998;* **Eleanor,** *18 inches, sculpted by Jan Hollebrands, edition of 2,500, 1994;* **Barbie Dawn,** *22 inches, sculpted by Beverly Stoehr, edition of 2,500, 1997;* **Amy San,** *15 inches, sculpted by Marie Osmond, edition of 1,500, 1998. All dolls are porcelain.*

BELOW RIGHT, BACK ROW, FROM LEFT:

Sonja, *20 inches, sculpted by Sonja Bryer, edition of 5,000, 1998;* **Nicolette,** *23 inches, sculpted by Beverly Stoehr, edition of 2,500, 1997.*

FRONT ROW, FROM LEFT:

Blue Boy, *17 inches, reproduction of Donny Osmond as Blue Boy, sculpted by Cindy Shafer, edition of 2,500, 1997;* **Pinky,** *17 inches, reproduction of Marie Osmond as Pinky, sculpted by Cindy Shafer, edition of 2,500, 1997. All dolls are porcelain.*

OPPOSITE PAGE, TOP, FROM LEFT:
The Nutcracker, *1996;* **Christmas Memories,** *1997;* **Little Drummer Boy,** *1997. All dolls are porcelain annual editions sculpted by Charlotte Bellsmith and 7 inches.*

OPPOSITE PAGE, BOTTOM, FROM LEFT:
Little Red Riding Hood, *1994;* **Alice in Wonderland,** *1998;* **Little Bo Peep,** *1994;* **Goldilocks,** *1995. All dolls are porcelain annual editions sculpted by Charlotte Bellsmith and 7 inches.*

ABOVE, FROM LEFT:
Cinderella, *1997;* **Beauty and The Beast,** *1996;* **Princess and The Pea,** *1995;* **Thumbelina,** *1996. All dolls are porcelain annual editions sculpted by Charlotte Bellsmith and 7 inches.*

SWEET DREAMS
Series

ABOVE, FROM LEFT:
Dawn, *porcelain, 23 inches, sculpted by Kathleen Fitzpatrick, edition of 5,000, 1997;* **Dream Baby,** *porcelain, 10 inches, Dream Baby reproduction, edition of 1,500, 1997*

RIGHT, FROM LEFT:
Baby Cuddles, *13½ inches, sculpted by Cheryl Robinson, edition of 1,500, 1996;* **Sweet Dreams Baby,** *13 inches, German reproduction, edition of 2,500, 1994;* **Olivia,** *7½ inches, Hilda reproduction, edition of 2,500, 1993. All dolls are porcelain.*

Lori Lavender,
*porcelain, 11 inches, sculpted
by Margie Costa, edition of
2,500, 1998*

Tea Cup Treasures,
porcelain, 4½ inches,
sculpted by Beverly Stoehr,
edition of 3,000, 1996

Terri Two-Two, *porcelain, 7 inches, sculpted by Michele Severino, edition of 5,000, 2000*

Donny and Marie, *porcelain, 11½ inches, sculpted by Sonja Bryer, edition of 20,000, 1998*

TINY TOTS
Series

TINY TOTS SERIES

RIGHT, FROM LEFT:
Chenoa, *5 inches, sculpted by Denise Krause, hand-numbered edition, 2000;* **Mato**, *5 inches, sculpted by Denise Krause, hand-numbered edition, 2001;* *(in sled)* **Cassidy**, *7 inches, sculpted by Sonja Bryer, hand-numbered edition, 1999;* *(in sled)* **Jingles & Belle**, *each 7 inches, sculpted by Beverly Stoehr, hand-numbered edition, 2000;* **I Love You Beary Much**, *7 inches, sculpted by Marie Osmond, bear by Annette Funicello, hand-numbered edition, 1999;* **Stephen**, *5 inches, sculpted by Beverly Stoehr, hand-numbered edition, 2000. All dolls are porcelain reduced versions of the original dolls.*

RIGHT, FROM LEFT:
Olive May, *sculpted by Marie Osmond, 1999;* **Baby Marie**, *sculpted by Beverly Stoehr, 1998;* **Baby Alexis**, *sculpted by Lisa Hatch;* **Ashley**, *sculpted by Beverly Stoehr. This is the original porcelain set of four Tiny Tots, produced in an edition of 20,000. Each doll is 7 inches seated.*

RIGHT, FROM LEFT:
Baby Marie's First Birthday, *7 inches, sculpted by Beverly Stoehr, hand-numbered edition, 1999;* **Debra**, *5½ inches, sculpted by Sonja Bryer, hand-numbered edition, 2000;* **Amaya**, *5 inches, sculpted by Sonja Bryer, hand-numbered edition, 2000;* **Lilly**, *7 inches, anonymous sculptor, open edition, 1999;* **Baby Miracles**, *7 inches, sculpted by Sonja Bryer, hand-numbered edition, 1999;* **Baby Megan**, *5 inches, sculpted by Beverly Stoehr, hand-numbered edition, 2000. All dolls are porcelain reduced versions of the original dolls.*

Baby Miss America, *porcelain,*
12 inches seated, sculpted by
Sonja Bryer, edition of 5,000, 2000

ABOVE, FROM LEFT:
Savannah Marie, *porcelain, 20 inches, sculpted by Marie Osmond, exclusive edition of 500 for Lane's Toyland, 1998;* **Leah,** *porcelain, 19½ inches, sculpted by Marie Osmond, exclusive edition of 2,500 for Lane's Toyland, 1997*

ABOVE RIGHT, FROM LEFT:
Jessica, *edition of 2,500, 1991;* **Jessica's First Christmas,** *edition of 5,000, 1993;* **Jessica's First Birthday,** *edition of 2,500, 1992. All dolls are porcelain, 23 inches, sculpted by Vincent De Filippo.*

RIGHT:
Ena, *porcelain, 15 inches, anonymous sculptor, edition of 5,000, 1999*

ABOVE, FROM LEFT:
Ashley, *porcelain, 23 inches, sculpted by Beverly Stoehr, edition of 5,000, 1995;* **Kristen**, *porcelain, 21 inches, sculpted by Brenda Connors, edition of 5,000, 1998*

LEFT, FROM LEFT:
Debbie, *23 inches, sculpted by Jan Hollebrands, 1993;* **Kayla**, *20 inches, sculpted by Diane Bucki, 2000;* **Suzanne**, *23 inches, sculpted by Maryse Nicole, year of introduction unknown. All dolls are porcelain editions of 2,500 each.*

Mato, *11 inches, sculpted by Denise Krause, edition of 2,500, 2000;* **Lilly**, *22 inches, anonymous sculptor, edition of 5,000, 1997;* **Very Beary in Love**, *19 inches, anonymous sculptor, edition of 2,500, 1999. All dolls are porcelain.*

Baby Marie Paper Roses, *edition of 5,000, 1997;* **Baby Marie Vinyl**, *edition of 2,500, 1998;* **Baby Marie Expo**, *edition of 350, 1998. All dolls are vinyl, 19½ inches and sculpted by Beverly Stoehr.*

FROM LEFT:
Saundra, *porcelain, 12 inches, anonymous sculptor, edition of 5,000, 1999;* **Debra**, *porcelain, 16 inches, sculpted by Sonja Bryer, edition of 2,500, 1998*

FROM LEFT:

Olive May Springtime, *edition of 7,500, 1997;* **Olive May Sunday Best,** *edition of 1,000, 2000;* **Olive May,** *edition of 20,000, 1995;* **Olive May Christmas,** *edition of 7,500, 1996. All dolls are porcelain, 24 inches, and sculpted by Marie Osmond.*

ABOVE, FROM LEFT:
Baby Marie's First Birthday, *porcelain,
21 inches, sculpted by Beverly Stoehr,
edition of 5,000, 1997;* **Baby Marie,**
*porcelain, 22 inches, sculpted by
Beverly Stoehr, edition of 5,000, 1996*

RIGHT:
Aleana, *porcelain, 19 inches, sculpted by
Marie Osmond, edition of 2,500, 1998*

RIGHT, FROM LEFT:
Ann Marie Holiday, *23 inches, edition of 5,000, 1998; (foreground)* **Santa Baby,** *12 inches seated, edition of 5,000, 1999;* **Cassidy,** *19 inches, edition of 2,500, 1998. All dolls are porcelain, and sculpted by Sonja Bryer.*

LEFT, FROM LEFT:
A Doll for All Seasons *(comes with Halloween and Christmas costumes), 2000.* **A Doll for All Seasons 2** *(comes with Easter and Fourth of July costumes), 2001. Both dolls are porcelain, 9½ inches, and sculpted by Michele Severino in an edition of 2,500 each.*

BELOW LEFT, FROM LEFT:
Victoria Leigh, *18 inches, sculpted by Marie Osmond, edition of 2,500, 1998;* **Mindy,** *16 inches, sculpted by Beverly Stoehr, edition of 2,000, 1999;* **Baby Beverly,** *16 inches, sculpted by Beverly Stoehr, edition of 5,000, 1995. All dolls are porcelain.*

BELOW:
Adriana, *porcelain,*
12 inches, sculpted by
Sonja Bryer, edition of
2,500, 2000

ABOVE RIGHT AND RIGHT:
Amaya, *porcelain, 12 inches,*
sculpted by Sonja Bryer, edi-
tion of 5,000, 1999

ABOVE, FROM LEFT:
Baby Marie Holiday Dress Up, *vinyl, 19½ inches, sculpted by Beverly Stoehr, edition of 100, 1998;* **Baby Marie Vinyl's First Christmas,** *vinyl with plush teddy bear, 19½ inches, sculpted by Beverly Stoehr, hand-numbered edition, 1999*

ABOVE RIGHT, FROM LEFT:
Daisy, *porcelain, 24 inches, sculpted by Marie Osmond, edition of 7,500, 1998;* **Peek-A-Boo,** *sculpted by Marie Osmond, bear by Annette Funicello, edition of 5,000, 1998*

ABOVE, FROM LEFT:
Baby Alexis Pretty in Pink, *porcelain, 21 inches, sculpted by Lisa Hatch, edition of 2,500, 1999;*
Sunshine and Happiness, *porcelain, 21 inches, sculpted by Beverly Stoehr, edition of 7,500, 1997;*
Mary Sunshine, *two-faced doll, porcelain, 15 inches, sculpted by Beverly Stoehr, edition of 2,500, 1998; (foreground, from left)* **Hannah Jo,** *porcelain, 9 inches, anonymous sculptor, edition of 5,000, 1999;* **Cherish Me Baby,** *vinyl, 10 inches, sculpted by Sonja Bryer, edition of 5,000, 1998*

Olive May, *porcelain, 24 inches, first doll sculpted by Marie Osmond, edition of 20,000, 1995*

FROM LEFT:
Trina; Tracy. *This set of two porcelain 9½-inch dolls was sculpted by Vincent De Filippo in a Disney exclusive edition of 250 in 1992. It does not belong to any series.*

RIGHT:
Sheila, *porcelain, 17 inches, sculpted by Berdine Creedy, edition of 2000, 1998*

BELOW, FROM LEFT:
Vanessa, *porcelain, 11 inches, Twirp reproduction, edition of 2,500, 1993;* **Tricia,** *porcelain, 16 inches, sculpted by Charlotte Bellsmith, edition of 2,500, 1992*

ORNAMENTS ON AND UNDER TREE:
12 Drummers Drumming, *4 inches;*
11 Pipers Piping, *4 inches;*
10 Lords-A-Leaping, *2½ inches;*
9 Ladies Dancing, *2½ inches;*
8 Maids-A-Milking, *3½ inches;*
7 Swans-A-Swimming, *3½ inches;*
6 Geese-A-Laying, *4 inches;*
5 Gold Rings, *4 inches;* **4 Calling Birds**, *2½ inches;* **3 French Hens**, *2½ inches;* **2 Turtle Doves**, *3½ inches;* **Partridge**, *3½ inches. All ornaments are porcelain and sculpted by Sonja Bryer in 1998.*

TWINS
Series

TWINS SERIES

RIGHT, FROM LEFT:
Rags *(out of wagon)* **& Rosie** *(in wagon, back row), 11 inches, annual edition, 1996;* **Baby Rags & Rosie,** *6½ inches, edition of 5,000, 2000;* **Jingles & Belle,** *11 inches, edition of 15,000, 1995;* **Rosie & Rags Clowning Around,** *8 inches, edition of 2,500, 1998;* **Rags & Mopsy,** *18 inches, edition of 5,000, 1994;* **Rosie & Rags as Mickey & Minnie,** *11 inches, annual edition, 1997. All dolls are porcelain and sculpted by Beverly Stoehr.*

BELOW:
Hansel & Gretel, *porcelain, 18 inches, sculpted by Beverly Stoehr, edition of 5,000, 1996*

146

Robbie Rabbit, *16 inches, 1993;* **Heavenly Hare,** *14½ inches, 1997;* **Rosemarie Rabbit,** *16 inches, 1994. All rabbits have porcelain faces, plush bodies and are editions of 5,000 each, sculpted by Linda Henry.*

Hareloom Bunny, *23 inches, 1994;* **Santa Bunny,** *21 inches, 1995;* **Mrs. Paws,** *21 inches, 1996. All rabbits have porcelain faces, plush bodies and are editions of 5,000 each, sculpted by Linda Henry.*

LEFT, FROM LEFT:
Fuzzy Baby & Hareiat,
8 inches and 7 inches,
sculpted by Linda Henry,
1996; **Blossom Bunny,**
21 inches, sculpted by
Linda Henry, 1995; **Velvet,**
22 inches, sculpted by
Linda Henry, 1992; **Rock-A-**
Bye Bunny, *20 inches,*
sculpted by Marie Osmond,
1998; (foreground) **Lots of**
Love Bunny, *10 inches,*
sculpted by Marie Osmond,
1999. All rabbits have
porcelain faces and plush
bodies, and are editions of
5,000 each.

LEFT, FROM LEFT:
Hula Hare, *10 inches,*
sculpted by Marie Osmond,
edition of 2,500, 1998;
Julienne Rabbit, *12 inches,*
sculpted by Linda Henry,
edition of 5,000, 1996; **Some**
Bunny to Love, *7½ inches*
and 4-inch chick, sculpted
by Marie Osmond and Lisa
Applebeary, edition of 5,000,
2000; **Kelly,** *12 inches,*
sculpted by Linda Henry,
edition of 5,000, 1995; (fore-
ground) **Kristi,** *17 inches,*
sculpted by Linda Henry,
edition of 5,000, 1995. All
rabbits have porcelain faces
and plush bodies.

FROM LEFT:
Grandma's Rose Garden;
Grandma's Storytime; Grandma's
Goodies. *All dolls are porcelain,
7 inches, sculpted by Sonja Bryer
in editions of 2,500 each and
introduced in 1999.*

FROM LEFT: **Toothfairy**, *porcelain, 9 inches, sculpted by Margie Costa, edition of 2,500, 1998;* **Darling Darlene**, *porcelain, 9 inches, sculpted by Margie Costa, edition of 2,500, 1998*

FROM LEFT:
Baby Cowardly Lion, *open edition, 1999;* **Baby Wicked Witch,** *open edition, 2000;* **Baby Dorothy,** *open edition, 1999;* **Baby Scarecrow,** *open edition, 1999;* **Baby Glinda the Good Witch,** *hand-numbered edition, 1999;* **Baby Tin Man,** *open edition, 1999. All dolls are porcelain, 12 inches and sculpted by Sonja Bryer.*

LEFT:
Disney Miracle Kids Adventure, *porcelain, 11 inches, sculpted by Linda Henry, one-of-a-kind sold at Disneyland Doll & Teddy Bear auction, 1993*

BELOW:
Southern Belle, *porcelain, 14 inches, sculpted by Marie Osmond, one-of-a-kind sold at Doll & Teddy Bear Expo East auction, 1997*

LEFT:
Laurel, *porcelain, 15 inches, sculpted by Beverly Stoehr, Disney exclusive edition of 40, 1997*

BELOW:
Jessica's Wedding Day, *porcelain, 28 inches, sculpted by Marie Osmond, one-of-a-kind sold at Disney World auction, 1997*

Isabel, *resin, 14 inches, sculpted by Carole Bowling, edition of 10, 2001*

155

ABOVE, FROM LEFT:
Maggie, *Toddler series, porcelain, 23 inches, sculpted by Jo Ann Pohlman, edition of 2,000;* **Abigail,** *Best Friends series, porcelain, 23 inches, sculpted by Kathleen Fitzpatrick, edition of 1,500*

ABOVE RIGHT:
Jillian, *Classics series, porcelain, 27 inches, sculpted by Mary Benner, edition of 500*

LEFT, FROM LEFT:
English Beefeater, *Small World series, 6½ inches, anonymous sculptor, Disneyland exclusive open edition; (in wagon)* **Rosie & Rags as Mickey & Minnie,** *Tiny Tots series, 5 inches, sculpted by Beverly Stoehr, open edition;* **Hawaiian Girl,** *Small World series, 6½ inches, anonymous sculptor, Disneyland exclusive open edition;* **Can Can Dancer,** *Small World series, 6½ inches, anonymous sculptor, Disneyland exclusive open edition*

LEFT, FROM LEFT:
Amaya Springtime, *Picture Day series, 12 inches, edition of 6,000;* **Baby Alice in Wonderland,** *Disney Babies series, 12 inches, open edition;* **Anniversary Angel Baby,** *New Millennium series, 12 inches, edition of 2,500. All dolls are porcelain and sculpted by Sonja Bryer.*

ABOVE, FROM LEFT:
Debbie, *Tiny Tots series, porcelain, 5 inches, sculpted by Jan Hollebrands, open edition;* **Trudi Two-Two,** *Terrific Two-Two series, porcelain, 7 inches, sculpted by Michele Severino, edition of 5,000; (foreground)* **Happy Fats,** *Collectibles series, porcelain, 3½ inches, Happy Fats reproduction, open edition;* **Sweet Settee,** *Home Décor series, porcelain, 7 inches, sculpted by Michael Everet, open edition;* **Cruisin',** *Little Me series, resin, 3½ inches, anonymous sculptor, open edition*

Remember Me, *Coming Up Roses series, porcelain, 24 inches, sculpted by Marie Osmond, edition of 20,000, 2001*

Index to The Collection